THE CONTINUING STORY
OF THE SPEAR OF DESTINY

Trevor Ravenscroft
&
Tim Wallace-Murphy

SAMUEL WEISER, INC.

York Beach, Maine

Published in 1997 by
Samuel Weiser, Inc.
P. O. Box 612
York Beach, ME 03910-0612

Library of Congress Cataloging-in-Publication Data:
    Ravenscroft, Trevor, 1921-1989.
        The mark of the beast : the continuing story of the Spear of Destiny
    / Tim Wallace-Murphy, Trevor Ravenscroft.
            p.   cm.
        Originally published: London : Sphere Books Ltd., 1990.
        Includes bibliographical references and index.
        ISBN 0-87728-870-4 (alk. paper)
            1. Holy Lance—Miscellanea. 2. Beast of the Apocalypse
    Miscellanea. 3. Six hundred and sixty-six (The number) in the Bible—
    Miscellanea. 4. Antichrist—Miscellanea. 5. End of the world—
    Miscellanea. I. Wallace-Murphy, Tim. II. Title.
    BF1442.H64W35   1997
    133.4'4—DC20   96-14629
                                                                  CIP

Exerpts from *The Aquarian Conspiracy* by Marilyn Ferguson are reproduced by
kind permission of Grafton Books, a division of the Collins Publishing Group.
Excerpts from *Brighter than a Thousand Suns* by Robert Jungk and translated by
James Cleugh were originally published by Schertz Verlag and are reproduced
by kind permission of Victor Gollancz Ltd.

Cover art by Ray Rue

Printed in the United States of America

BJ

04 03 02 01
10 9 8 7 6 5 4 3

CONTENTS

SECTION 3

THE SEEDS OF TERROR

SECTION 4

LIFE IN THE SHADOW OF THE PALE HORSE

SECTION 5

GATHERING AT THE THRESHOLD

SECTION 6

THE PROPHESIED FUTURE?

PROLOGUE

*Now it was the day of Preparation,
and the next day was to be a special
Sabbath. Because the Jews did not want
the bodies left on the crosses during the
Sabbath, they asked Pilate to have the
legs broken and the bodies taken down.*

*The soldiers therefore came and broke
the legs of the first man who had been
crucified with Jesus, and then those of
the other. But when they came to Jesus
and found that he was already dead, they
did not break his legs.*

*Instead, one of the soldiers pierced
Jesus' side with a spear, bringing a
sudden flow of blood and water.*

*The man who saw it has given testimony,
and his testimony is true. He knows that
he tells the truth, and he testifies so
that you also may believe.*

*These things happened so that the
Scripture would be fulfilled. 'Not one of
his bones will be broken,' and, as
another scripture says, 'They will
look on the one they have pierced.'*

The Gospel of St John (New International
Version):19, verses 31–37

INTRODUCTION

The Spear of Longinus rests in the *Weltliche Schatzkammer* in the Hofburg in Vienna. The talisman of world historic destiny stands òn a faded red velvet dais within an open leather case in exactly the same place in the treasure house where Adolf Hitler first beheld it in 1909. Since *The Spear of Destiny* was first published in 1972 and gained a world-wide readership in seventeen foreign editions, hundreds of thousands of people have made a special visit to the Hofburg to see the Holy Lance which is associated with so strange a legend.

This legend first arose when the Roman Centurion Gaius Cassius Longinus pierced the side of Jesus Christ on the cross to prevent the mutilation which was the fate of the two thieves who hung from the crosses on either side of him. Longinus became a hero of the first Christians because they believed that the resurrection as we know it could not have been accomplished if the bones of Christ had been shattered contrary to the mysterious prophecy of Isaiah 'a bone of him shall not be broken.' It was said that the Roman Centurion had for a moment in time held the destiny of the whole of mankind in his hands. It was for this reason that the lance became known as 'The Spear of Destiny' and became one of the great treasures of Christendom. The legend, gaining strength with the passing of the centuries, tells that whoever possesses it and understands the powers it serves holds the destiny of the world in his hands for good or evil.

The role of the Spear did not end with the recorded history of its claimants which were described in the first volume of this work. Nor must it be allowed to remain the

1

exclusive interest of the leaders of nations seeking to wield its powers. Its true significance for our time rests with each and every individual who seeks to understand the meaning of their own unfolding destiny in this apocalyptic age.

The coming apocalyptic decades will see the emergence of a World Dictator whose global rule will be harnessed to the evil powers also associated with the Spear. And this new Leviathan can only eventually be overthrown by the resistance of spiritually orientated individuals for there will be no armies or States to oppose him. If this appears incredible, then think only of the moment when Adolf Hitler first saw the Spear of Destiny in 1909 and vowed that it would become his talisman of power for world conquest. Nobody at that time would have believed that within two decades an alien civilization would arise in central Europe which would substitute the swastika for the Cross and evoke the greatest holocaust the world had ever seen. The next forty years will see far more horrendous events on an apocalyptic scale. For those who are aware of the real meaning behind the changing scenes of our time there are already clear signs of the coming global events that will change the face of history.

The same powers which have been traditionally associated with the claimants to the Lance of Longinus and the initiates of the Grail can be developed by any concerned individual in the present age who seeks them. We describe the most recent changes in the evolution of human consciousness which have opened the spiritual realities symbolized by the Spear to all mankind. A section of this book describes these newly emerging faculties, how they can be developed and what insights they yield. These very faculties have been used in the latter half of the twentieth century to recapture the spiritual insight of the Chartres Masters of the Middle Ages to discover how they secretly built a prophetic calendar in stone which precisely dates the critical phase of the Apocalypse at the end of the present century.

The purpose of this second volume is to enable you the reader to use the powers of the Spear to gain a new and deeper insight into the unfolding pattern of your own life; and at the same time interpret the symbolism of the Revelation of St John so that it becomes a magic mirror revealing the dread countenance of the Apocalypse within the unfolding fabric of contemporary and coming events in which all our personal destinies are inextricably woven. The drama and symbolism of history is itself the result of such interweaving of human reincarnation patterns. The spiritual biographies of leading personalities unveil the working of the law of Karma and describe the former incarnations of the physicists who created the atomic bomb.

Using these very faculties associated with the Spear of Destiny we will interpret the strange mythological symbolism of the Revelation of St John in everyday, rational and scientific terms. And in such a manner describe the nature of the coming global catastrophes at the commencement of the epoch which will culminate in the appearance of the Great Dictator and Anti-Christ.

SECTION 1

FROM GOLGOTHA TO HIROSHIMA

The Spear as Key to History

The mould of the legend was created by the history of a chain of illustrious claimants to the Spear throughout two thousand years who were aware of its magical powers to shape the destiny of mankind.

The Spear became the talisman for Adolf Hitler who harnessed its powers in an attempt to conquer the world. The detailed history of Hitler's rise to power and the black occultism of the Nazi party were recorded in the first volume of this work which unveiled how even the process of genocide was an integral part of the dedicated service to evil powers in the first phase of the Apocalypse.

Not even the Holocaust and the Nazi reign of terror were enough to awaken mankind to the awareness that Adolf Hitler was the vessel for the first appearance of the Beast from the Abyss prophesied in the Revelation of St John.

Hitler was the first non-royal claimant to the Spear of Longinus and ended the significance of the bloodline of the Kings who had guided the destiny of the separate nations in the formation of Europe. In the era of the present confrontation of the opposing ideologies of East and West, mankind is unwittingly hurled against the threshold of the spiritual world. It is at this very threshold that each individual must become aware of and identify the twofold face of evil which threatens both the spiritual and the physical existence of the world we live in.

The symbolism of the Four Horses of the Apocalypse indicates the radical changes in the thinking of mankind against the background of the millennia. The emergence over the horizon of history of the Pale Horse whose rider is Death signifies the beginning of the atomic age when the United States of America became custodians of the Spear of Destiny and unleashed the atom bomb on Hiroshima.

CHAPTER ONE

THE SPEAR AT THE THRESHOLD OF THE NEW AGE

The solitary iron spearhead black with age still rests on a faded red velvet dais within an open leather case. Its long tapering point is supported by a wide base with metal flanges depicting the wings of a dove. Within a central aperture of the blade a hammer-headed nail is secured by a cuff threaded with gold, silver and copper wire. On the side of the lowest portion of the base golden crosses are embossed.

The Spear of Destiny has an altogether different presence to the crowns, sceptres and other rich and gaudy paraphernalia on display in the Treasure House in the Hofburg in Vienna. The various items of royal regalia are but mementoes of a bygone age. The Spear of Longinus however is no mere historical artifact but a resonator of great spiritual power as relevant to the destiny of mankind today as it was when the Roman Centurion Gaius Cassius pierced the side of Christ with it two thousand years ago.

The illustrious claimants to the Spear throughout two thousand years were aware of its magical powers to shape the destiny of mankind. Today these powers are no longer the sole preserve of an élite chain of good and evil initiates, but belong to each and every human being of any race or creed who seeks to understand them. Any sensitive human soul who beholds the Spear today and becomes aware of its powers finds himself at the threshold between the terrestrial world and the spiritual world. This dramatic change in the

7

role of the Spear has been brought about by the Spirit of the Time to enable each individual to face and understand the working of good and evil in the apocalyptic age which has already begun.

Because mankind now stands at the very threshold of the spiritual world, the purpose of this volume is to enable the reader to understand the spiritual powers behind the Spear in order to gain a new and deeper insight into the unfolding pattern of his life. It will also serve to interpret the symbolism of the Revelation of St John and to transform it into a magic mirror revealing the dread countenance of the Apocalypse within the unfolding fabric of contemporary and coming events.

Few people yet realize that the first phase of the Apocalypse began in the opening years of this century at the time when the young Adolf Hitler stood before the Spear of Destiny in the Hofburg. This moment of insight enabled him to lift the veil to perceive how he could harness its powers to rule the world. Thirty years later Adolf Hitler, now Führer of the German Reich, conquered Austria and became the successor to the Habsburg Emperors. On this occasion when he entered the treasure house there were no guards, petty officials or attendants to keep a suspicious and wary eye as there were when he first saw the Spear as an unkempt outcast. Now he was free to remove the ancient weapon from its faded red velvet dais behind protecting glass. One can only presume that he held the Talisman of Power in his own hands, feeling the black metal of the tapering point which two thousand years before had pierced the side of Christ at the crucifixion.

It was surely a scene which that genius of the bizarre, Charlie Chaplin himself, would never have dared to stage. And yet it was a happening so potent with evil that it would cause an eruption more violent and destructive than the entire world had ever known: a happening which caused the first incendiary flicker of a merciless 'Will to Power' that would quickly spread in blazing desolation to turn a whole continent to rubble. An unseen communing with dark Principalities and Powers which would inspire a demonic reign of terror and cold-blooded butchery outstripping in primitive savagery and bestial cruelty all previous ages of tyranny and oppression in the entire history of mankind.

This very night when Hitler secretly claimed the Spear of Destiny was to become known in Vienna as 'The Night of Terror'. He left the treasure house to initiate a most dreadful pogrom against the Jewish population and some one-hundred-thousand Jews were arrested. Such were the scenes of sadism and brutality in the streets of the city that many Jews even fled into Germany itself to find refuge. A new concentration camp was set up on the north bank of the Danube which was to earn an infamous reputation – Mauthausen. Here the official execution list was to be longer than any other camp within the confines of the Reich. It was revealed at the Nuremberg trials that the decision to go ahead with the plans for the 'final solution' dated from that night. For Adolf Hitler this was the night of decision. He no longer needed instruments of guile and political cunning for he now used the powers of the Spear as a catalyst and became completely ensouled by the Leviathan who struck out openly to achieve the ultimate aim – the conquest of the world.

The conflict which came a year later quickly became global in its effects as no other previous war had ever done, not only involving the belligerents but also every nation in the world including those who remained neutral. No one was exempt from its reach. Entire civilian populations were subject not only to the terrors of aerial bombardment but also to the deliberate and calculated policy of genocide. The concept of crimes against humanity resulting from these events led to the Nuremberg trials where for the first time leaders of defeated nations were arraigned. Yet these trials failed to identify the nature of the evil at work behind the outer façade of National Socialism.

The Allied prosecutors apparently lacked the moral imagination to perceive the apocalyptic countenance of the civilization which had arisen in Germany between the two world wars – a civilization based on a magical *Weltanschauung* which had substituted the Swastika for the Cross. It appears there was a unanimous agreement among the judges to treat the accused as an integral part of the humanist and Cartesian system of the western world. This was the outward reinforcement of a deliberate and covert political decision taken at the highest level to explain the most atrocious crimes in history as a result of mental aberration. It was thought expedient to speak in dry psychoanalytical terms when considering their motives for incarcerating millions of human beings in gas ovens rather than to reveal that such practices were an integral part of a dedicated service to evil powers.

To have admitted even for an instant what their defeated enemies were really like, to have lifted the veil to reveal the real motives for such an astonishing reversal of values would have opened millions of people to the risk of a terrible corruption. In such a way the real apocalyptic countenance of the twentieth century was deliberately kept hidden from the masses. It remains so to this day! And this is why the first phase of the twentieth-century Apocalypse came upon us without its warning identity being revealed.

As if this were not tragedy enough, the next phase has already begun and will culminate in another attempt by the Leviathan to take over the planet:

> One of the heads of the Beast seemed to have had a fatal wound, but the fatal wound had been healed. The whole world was astonished and followed the Beast.

This new and yet more critical phase of the apocalyptic age will be characterized by disasters and chaos culminating in the reappearance of the Beast who will ensoul the coming World Dictator and achieve world conquest where Hitler failed.

The Beast was given a mouth to utter proud words and blasphemies and to exercise his authority ... He was given power to make war against the saints and to conquer them. And he was given authority over every tribe, people, language and nation. All inhabitants of the earth will worship the Beast.

The Revelation of St John (New International Version): 13, verses 5–8

CHAPTER TWO

THE SPEAR AS SYMBOL OF THE APOCALYPSE

The masses of humanity are as yet totally unaware of the spiritual realities that they now must consciously confront. They stand unknowingly at the threshold. Not even the events of this century so far have awakened them: for them physical life is always completely absorbing and usually exhausting. The masses in their blindness have become hopeless victims of a whole series of world disasters and today they stand bewildered and alarmed and ready to panic into any plausible policy of violence. It is the tragedy of the ordinary man that he never listens to the warnings of the prophets until doom is upon him, and then he is too terrified to listen and too stupefied to understand, and in any case too late. One would have thought that he would need no prophet to convince him that he is faced with world catastrophe and disaster. The problem is that the average person is unable to read the changing scenes of the times. Even when the whole civilization of Europe lay in ruins, across which the two colossi of East and West growled alarmingly at one another in the aftermath of World War II, the man in the street was quite unable to see that humanity had already passed through the first phase of the Apocalypse – the Hitler era of the Seven-Horned Beast.

The science, invention, organization and techniques of the twentieth century have opened up boundless possibilities for the widespread comfort of mankind. Yet, besides these great benefits, the present technological age has brought in its wake modes of pollution and weapons of destruction that threaten the extinction of all life on this planet.

An increasing number of intelligent people feel a growing unease that this nuclear age is charged with a spiritual significance far more riveting than any previous historical time. Many such people, who have recognized how our century is becoming increasingly apocalyptic in character, have sought guidance from the Book of Revelation of St John, the Divine, but have been quite unable to interpret its strange symbolism. For what sense can the rational mind make of this mysterious work which describes the destiny of mankind in terms of Seals, Trumpet Blasts and Vials of Wrath, Winged Horsemen and Beasts from the Abyss? With the utmost goodwill what can the rational mind make of such unworldly pictures. Modern thinking with its dialectic materialism and cold computer calculation, which reduces even man himself to a statistical cypher, can only regard the visionary symbolism of the Revelation as crass superstition, bizarre to the point of absurdity or, at best, the outworn mythology of an age long past.

Last century it was the Russian philosopher Soloviev who wrote a prophetic book on the Anti-Christ inspired by the Book of Revelation. Living at the dawn of the Apocalypse, Soloviev's Anti-Christ is no mythical figure but inhabits the soul of a man of flesh and blood in everyday reality. A man dressed in ordinary clothes and outwardly so inconspicuous that he could pass unnoticed in a crowd. Soloviev saw that the greatest danger would be just this: 'The Beast doesn't look what he is.' He is young and vigorous and his voice rings out with magical power which, like the seductive tones of the pied piper, can seduce great leaders into a terrifying condition of diminished responsibility, and at the same time excite the masses to rise up and turn a dying culture into a heap of rubble and ashes. Beneath a banal and disarming exterior – 'He may even wear a comic moustache' – he is a blood-hungry tyrant and a mighty demagogue.

Soloviev's Leviathan does not take over the soul and the body of a Jew as the Nazis falsely proclaimed. On the contrary, he had the insight to see that precisely the most enlightened Jews, retaining the piety of their age-old wisdom, would be among the few people who identified and denounced the Beast before he sought to conquer the world. Soloviev also foresaw that it would be the Jewish race who would be the victims of the dreadful pogrom initiated by the Anti-Christ. He includes in his shattering prophecies even such details and descriptions of how the skins of the Jews would be turned into household articles, just as it came to pass in the concentration camps of the Third Reich in which swaggering SS murdered their Jewish slaves and used their skins to make table lamps.

The date in which Soloviev predicted these things should come to pass? 1921! The age of this human vehicle of hell? Thirty-three years old! Adolf Hitler celebrated his thirty-third birthday in 1921, the year he assumed the uncontested leadership of the National Socialist party.

Hermann Rauschning, a Nazi *gauleiter* who defected to the West, recognized Adolf Hitler as the first appearance of the Beast of the Revelation. Rauschning, an authentic biographer of the Führer, entitled one of his books *The Beast from the Abyss*. Rauschning knew that Hitler had abandoned himself to forces which were carrying him away – apocalyptic forces of dark and destructive violence. 'Hitler imagined that he still had freedom of choice but he had long been in bondage to a magic which might well have been described, not only in metaphor but in literal fact, as that of Evil Hierarchies of Spirits. Instead of a man emerging step by step from the obscurity of youth, and freeing himself from its dross on an upward course, we witnessed the development of a man possessed, the helpless prey to

14

powers of darkness.'

The most revealing flash of insight into Hitler as a vessel of the Beast was found in a poem written by a man who was executed for his part in the plot to assassinate the Führer. The poet was Major Albrecht Haushofer whose father initiated Hitler into the Secret Doctrine. The sonnet entitled 'The Father' recalls an ancient legend of the Orient which bears a striking resemblance to a verse in the Book of Revelation: 'When the thousand years are over Satan will be released from his prison' (Chapter 20, verse 7).

Albrecht Haushofer had learned about this ancient legend on a pre-war journey to Tibet. Apparently according to this legend the Spirits of Unholy Powers were incarcerated and sealed countless fathoms below in the darkness of the ocean. There they remained imprisoned by the beneficent hand of God, until, *once in a thousand years*, it was fated that a fisherman had it within his free choice to release the dreaded Beast unless he cast his terrible catch straight back into the depths.

> For my Father the lot was cast.
> Once again the demon had to be repulsed
> And thrust back into his prison.
> My father broke the seal –
> He sensed not the breath of the Evil One
> But set him free to roam the world.

These primitive insights arose in men who were not themselves able to relate the symbolism of the Apocalypse to the historical process. Their problem was that they were unable to perceive the indications given in a hidden manner within the pages of the Revelation itself as to when and how the most critical phase of the Apocalypse would take place. The clue rests in the order of appearance of·'The Four Horsemen of The Apocalypse', the most widely known and the least understood symbols of the Revelation.

15

The Revelation is by nature a form of mythology predicting the future destiny of mankind using the symbolism of its own time, and the horse which figured so prominently in all ancient mythology represented human intelligence. Presumably this came about because the horse was so closely linked to the development of man and the civilizations he inhabited. Anyway, the horse was considered to be the most intelligent of beasts. St John himself regarded the horse as an outward physical symbol of human intelligence and projects four striking examples of the horse to indicate the changing nature and quality of human consciousness throughout history.

'The Four Horses of The Apocalypse' represent four critical stages in the quality of human consciousness and the very nature of thinking which have taken place during the last five thousand years. These four stages in the evolution of human consciousness are like four great arches across the millennia through which the faculty of thinking has passed in its descent from universal mind to individual man. If we can identify in succession each of these crucial changes, we will be able to date precisely the Holocaust which is predicted to take place under the sinister symbolism of 'The Pale Horse' at the very threshold of a new and more enlightened age.

> And I saw, and behold a white horse: and he that sat on him had a bow; and a crown was given unto him: and he went forth conquering and to conquer.
>
> Revelation (King James Version): 6, verse 2

The White Horse appears at the moment in the drama of human evolution when man and nature were still entwined in an apparently celestial condition and, since there was not yet any sign of individual human consciousness, the curtain was not yet raised on history. For history belongs only to the human being and not to natural beings and natural events; nor did it arise in the case of man until his consciousness had evolved so far that he could make a personal response to the impact of nature. It was the masterpiece of evolution to produce a being who organically belongs entirely to the natural process of the world, but whose consciousness has become detached from that process and is able to look on natural events. History takes up the tale where evolution leaves off.

St John in his mystical insight seems to be indicating that the White Horse and its Rider symbolize man who is both clairvoyant and clairaudient but still without any form of consciousness of his own; man who shared unconsciously in a thinking which was the prerogative of higher intelligence. The long epoch of the White Horse begins to come to an end between 4000 and 3000 BC. It is typified by the various peoples living in that vast territory known today as the Middle East. The crucial change happened in a startling transformation of consciousness as man ceased to be a puppet of the gods and came into a sharper and more clearly defined awareness of the world around him, leaving him totally unaware of the sublime reality which had once been his natural but unconscious birthright.

Here we pass across the arch of the millennia from dying mythological history to Athens where in Ancient Greece the Red Horseman of the Apocalypse first appears.

And there went out another horse that was red: and power was given to him that sat thereon to take peace from the earth, and that they should kill one another: and there was given unto him a great sword.

Ibid., verse 4

The colour of this horse depicts thinking tinged with human blood because man has absorbed into his own soul

17

what was formerly inspired from outside him. The Red Horse seems to symbolize universal intelligence which has now become humanized into individual thinking. Those ancient faculties out of which mythology was born now wane. The fate of mankind which once rested in the hands of the gods now passes to individual men who become the masters of their own destiny. But just because man now had the capacity to weave his own thoughts, the possibility of human error arose. This is why the rider of the Red Horse brandishes a great sword and why he is given the power to cause strife among men.

The Red Horse first appeared on the historical horizon in 700 BC at the very beginning of the Greco–Roman age, but it wasn't until the fifth century BC in Greece that we find an individualized human thinking immediately concerned with everyday problems of life. For the first time man's own creative powers blossomed forth in art and architecture, in drama, in oratory and in politics. Above all it was logic which came into its own, a thinking based entirely on the working of the human mind as exemplified by the categories of Aristotle who first interposed reflection between perceptual stimulus and response. This type of thinking was to last for more than two thousand years until the emergence of the Black Horse in the fifteenth century AD.

> And I beheld, and lo a black horse; and he that sat on him had a pair of balances in his hand. And I heard a voice in the midst of the four beasts say, A measure of wheat for a penny, and three measures of barley for a penny; and see thou hurt not the oil and the wine.
>
> *Ibid.*, verses 5–6

The Black Horse seems to have established itself above the arena of European history by the beginning of the sixteenth century when sense-derived thinking takes hold of western

man to bring the dawn of the age of science and materialism. There was never any doubt in the Greek mind that
thinking was concerned with a *real* world of ideas. The
substance of thought – ideas – was far more real than the
substance of the phenomenal world. Thinking, alone and
unaided, could attain to the Good, the Beautiful and the
True. This belief in the intrinsic ability of thinking to reach
ultimate truth permeated deeply, though with growing
doubts, into the Middle Ages.

The last remnant of this type of awareness, with its
intimations of the existence of a moral order in the universe
found no place within the new and materialistic urge
towards scientific investigation. Although thinking came to
be regarded as arising solely from the physical brain, man
observed the world around him with far clearer definition
and as a result became more intensely aware of himself as
object, his self consciousness in this way becoming enormously enhanced. The whole mood of this new age of the
Black Horse expressed itself in the famous words of Francis
Bacon, the father of modern science: 'Reality only presents
itself to us when we look upon the world of the senses. The
senses alone provide us with realities, the realities of empirical knowledge.' The new age of inductive reasoning was
under way and man became very quickly at home with the
forces of the physical world which now separated him from
all former awareness of his own spiritual origin and isolated
his individual consciousness in an apparently godless
world. However it was only through such apparent isolation
from all presence of the Divine that man could attain
personal freedom – that freedom without which there can
be no love.

The power of thinking has now descended yet further
with the appearance of the Pale Horse passing beyond the
realm of materialism, and the individual capacity to love,
into sub-human spheres. St John uses the first three horses

to depict how Divine intelligence descends to the human level but with the appearance of the Pale Horse he warns us human intelligence is in danger of becoming demonic.

And I looked, and behold a pale horse: and his name that sat on him was Death, and Hell followed with him. And power was given unto them over the fourth part of the earth, to kill with sword, and with hunger, and with death, and with the beasts of the earth.

Ibid., verse 8

The Pale Horse denotes thinking which has turned into cold inhuman abstraction – the kind of uprooted and ruthless thinking which can create nuclear weapons in the name of the advancement of science while caring nothing for the threat it involves to all life on the planet. The Pale Horse represents the statistics of the 'overkill' in which human life is merely a cypher to be programmed into the computer.

The history of the Spear as the central symbol of the Apocalypse, whether its powers were used for good or evil, reveals the true and false aims of mankind throughout the two millennia of Christendom. It is for this reason no coincidence that America came into possession of this fateful talisman and was the unwitting claimant to its powers when the first atom bombs were dropped on Hiroshima and Nagasaki initiating the era of the Pale Horse.

The United States of America became the new claimant to the Spear of Destiny at 2.10 p.m. on 30 April 1945. This was the moment when Adolf Hitler shot himself in the bunker beneath the ruins of the Reich Chancellery in Berlin. It was also the moment when the US Army Intelligence, 'Section Five', discovered the Spear hidden in a vault beneath Nuremberg castle. While American soldiers of the

Third Division held the Spear under twenty-four-hour guard in Nuremberg, the *Enola Gay* dropped the first atom bomb on Hiroshima. Like the sorcerer's apprentice the United States had unleashed powers it could not control. The age of the Pale Horse, whose rider is Death and whose followers are the Hosts of Hell, had emerged over the horizon of history.

Whereas the first volume of this work described the history of how the powers of the Spear were directed throughout the historical epochs of the Red and the Black Horses, this second volume will outline the struggle by the leaders of nations to control and direct the powers of the Spear under the dread countenance of the Pale Horse.

CHAPTER THREE

THE SPEAR AND THE DESTINY OF NATIONS

Phineas, the ancient prophet, caused the Spear to be forged to symbolize the magical powers inherent in the blood of God's Chosen People – the people who were destined through the descending generations of their blood to prepare a body for the coming Messiah. It had already become such a vital symbol by the time of Herod the Great that he held it as his insignia of power over life and death when he ordered the massacre of the innocent babes throughout Judea in order to slay the Christ Child who would grow up to be called the King of the Jews. It was also carried by the captain of the Temple Guard as a symbol of his authority to break the bones of Jesus Christ. Snatching the weapon from the hands of the Israelite captain, Gaius Cassius Longinus performed the fateful act which gave rise to the present legend of the Spear of Destiny.

In some strange and inexplicable manner, this moment when Longinus held the destiny of the world in his hands coincided with the first stirring of the tribes in the north of Europe and across Russia who began their gradual and warlike migrations southwards towards Rome which in those days was the centre of the known world.

Another event which seemed to predict the future development of Europe happened at Pentecost when the Spirit descended on the disciples in the upper room. The Gospels describe how they went forth 'speaking with tongues' which at that time none could understand. A western occult tradition tells how the twelve disciples, each of whom came from a separate tribe within the Jewish race, were speaking the future languages of the twelve main peoples of Europe – an unwitting prophecy that the future folksouls of the nations of Europe would become Christian. Thirty years later with the Diaspora of the Jewish people and the destruction of their temple the stage was set for the eventual Christianization of the Roman Empire.

A giant stride towards the Christianization of Rome took place when the Emperor Diocletian gathered his armies for a pagan festival aimed at renewing the waning fervour of the legions for the pantheon of Roman Gods. Mauritius, the commander of the Theban Legion who were all Christians, refused to worship the Roman gods in whom he no longer believed. As a result he was decapitated in front of his own troops, who elected to follow his example and, divesting themselves of their weapons, knelt to bare their necks for slaughter. This martyrdom of the Theban Legion, at that time the holders of the Spear of Destiny and the most disciplined troops in the history of the Roman Army, softened the underbelly of pagan Rome and paved the way for the meteoric career of Constantine the Great and the conversion of the Roman Empire to Christianity.

Constantine held the Spear as a talisman of power at the decisive battle on the Milvian Bridge giving him control of the entire Roman Empire which by his decree became Christian. Thus Constantine the Great became the first 'Holy Roman Emperor', but sadly his motives were to use Christianity solely for the perpetuation of the martial aims of the Roman State. This tragic error transformed a religion of love and passive resistance into a form of militant imperialism in which nation would confront nation throughout the coming centuries in bitter wars each convinced that *God was with them.*

The Spear played its role through the centuries of the

decline of the Roman Empire, both in resisting the invasions and in converting the barbarians to the new faith. In the hands of the Frankish leader Karl Martel, the Hammer, the Spear inspired the victory at Poitiers which turned back the Arab invasion of Europe. Charlemagne found his whole dynasty on the Spear and its legend of world historic destiny in the ninth century which witnessed the final decline of Roman culture and the first emergence of the nations of Europe. In Britain, Alfred the Great, who had conquered the Danes, now began translating Latin works into the English idiom and laying the foundations of an island nation; Norway had its first king and the Danes also were united under a single sovereign; the commerce of the city of Utrecht was preparing the way for the emergence of Holland. Even the foundations of modern Russia were laid in this century when Rurik, the Norseman, became the first prince of Novgorod.

The grandfather of Charlemagne, Charibert of Leon, was an initiate of the Grail Order and possessed penetrating clairvoyant powers. He perceived with great clarity the benign spirit associated with the Holy Lance. He passed on his clairvoyance to his descendants and his bloodline did not lose its importance when the Carolingian Empire fell into decadence. Nearly all the royal families which for a thousand years have worn the crowns of the separate nations of Europe have a genealogical link to the Carolingian Dynasty whose power was based on the possession of the Spear of Longinus.

As the tribes and peoples merged in their various localities in the ninth century the folksouls gave birth to the languages and characters of the individual nations whose Royal Houses were to last for a thousand years. Each folksoul gradually brought into being a distinct national character with a unique temperament and destiny. Each nation acquired its own specific and distinct outlook, attri-

24

butes and capacities, creating its separate identity and sense of purpose and mission which contributed to the overall culture of the European Continent.

The powers of the Spear during these centuries served the interests of the whole of Europe which went beyond the special interests of the individual nations. Henry of Burgundy held the Spear at the battle of Lech where the invading Magyars were defeated outside Vienna. The defeated Magyars themselves later founded the Hungarian nation thus extending the boundaries of civilized Europe and making a distinct contribution to the emerging European culture. King Athelstan of England used the powers of the Spear in a similar manner to vanquish the Danes at the battle of Malmesbury thus concluding the work of consolidation begun by Alfred the Great. Athelstan in turn gave the Spear of Destiny to Otto the Great on condition that the German Emperor turned the fortress towns of Europe into trading cities in order to expand the economy of Europe.

One has only to read Winston Churchill's *History of the Island Nation* to perceive the sequential phases of the life of the English folksoul which first brought the separate peoples together around Alfred the Great and began to weld them into a nation. Under its guidance the language, literature, architecture and customs which gave the English people their unique and distinct character began to emerge. As the folksoul matured so did the nation, bringing about the unity of the separate peoples of the British Isles under a developing and democratic and unwritten constitution. A later phase in the fulfilment of the folksoul saw the building of the British Empire.

The final task of the English folksoul was the conquest of Nazi Germany and those who can remember the inspired speeches of Winston Churchill felt that the folk spirit of the nation spoke through him. Churchill also lived to see the conclusive act of the folksoul in handing back a vast empire to its many separate peoples, who now form the Common-wealth of nations each having inherited a constitution and system of justice based on the English model. At the state funeral of Sir Winston Churchill the last representatives of the royal families of Europe along with many heads of state failed to recognize that they were not only mourning the death of the great wartime leader but also the ultimate departure of the folksoul of the nation. The Duke of Norfolk, hereditary Earl Marshal of England, later commented that this occasion marked the final demise of national pageantry.

Strangely, it was an American who compared the folk-souls of the nations to people. Nations, said President Roosevelt, have a body which must be housed, clothed and fed; a soul which must be nourished and a spirit to fulfil the common aims of the people. He could have added that folk-souls, like people, also pass through developmental phases of youthful vigour, adolescence, maturity, sickness and decline. The greatest cause of sickness and decline of the folksouls in Europe arose through forms of false patriotism engendered by the idea that God himself could be identi-fied with the aims of the nation and that the rights of every individual had to be subjugated to this supposedly 'Divine Right of Kings' supported by the hereditarily privileged class of the nobility. The first great upheaval against this mistaken attitude was the French Revolution in which the rallying cry was 'Liberté, Égalité, Fraternité'. Sadly the revolution merely replaced the tyranny of the 'Divine Right of Kings' with the tyranny of mob rule and the chaotic period known simply as 'The Terror'. Out of this period of chaos arose a figure of Destiny, a Corsican General, Napoleon Bonaparte.

Napoleon, thinking it was his destiny to conquer the world, intended to substitute members of his own family and his entourage for the hereditary crowned heads of

Europe. To further this aim he attempted to seize the Spear which at that time was on display in St Katherine's Church in Nuremberg. The Holy Lance was removed by the *Germanenorden*, an occult lodge that understood the powers associated with the Spear, before the Emperor could get his hands on it in order to harness the talisman to his own ambitions. A member of the same Order attempted to assassinate Napoleon while he was inspecting his guards at Schömbrunn. The Spear was handed over to the Habsburg dynasty who refused to return it to Germany at the end of the Napoleonic wars. Unaware of its powers, the Habsburg Emperors merely kept it as part of the *Reichsheiligtümer*, the holy relics which were on display alongside the crown jewels in the Treasure House in the Hofburg.

Kaiser Wilhelm of Germany set up an elaborate ruse in 1913 to bring the Spear into his own immediate possession, his advisers telling him that there was an ancient royal decree that the Holy Lance should rest eternally in the Fatherland. An exhibition of Germanic art was staged in Berlin and Emperor Franz Joseph of Austria was invited to attend this exhibition in person on a state visit. On these grounds the Kaiser requested the temporary loan of the ancient holy relics of the German Emperors which had been spirited out of Nuremberg at the time of Napoleon. The ruse failed when members of the German General Staff, fearing their monarch's bellicose ambitions, warned Franz Joseph of the real motive for Wilhelm's sudden uncharacteristic interest in German art. Less than a year later the First World War began.

Ahead stretched four years of mortal combat in the shell-pitted wastes and leafless stumps of Flanders. The only hope left to the soldiers of all nations who lived through the murderous deadlock was the forlorn hope that they were fighting a 'war to end all wars'. Millions of 'sleeping' men were confronting one another in a prolonged nightmare of death and mutilation in the veritable Hades of trench warfare. The great fear in the hearts of these men of all nationalities was the same – the dread of a spiritual awakening through which they would see that all their cherished patriotic ideals were no more than a deadly tissue of dreams. Only long-drawn-out war of unprecedented magnitude and suffering could awaken mankind to the falsity of its beliefs and values and at the same time kill off the sons of the ruling classes that had propagated them.

The destruction of the hereditary ruling élite was given greater impetus by the machinations of Germany's war leaders who, in order to remove the threat of the Russian army, enabled Lenin to journey to Moscow in the 'sealed train' to instigate the Bolshevik revolution. This attempt by a materialistic ideology to impose from above the concept of equal opportunity and human rights was as doomed and tyrannical as the system it soon replaced. In the aftermath of the Great War it became apparent that ideologies had begun to replace the power and authority held for a thousand years by the successive royal claimants to the Spear since the reign of Charlemagne.

The first non-royal claimant to the Spear of Destiny was Adolf Hitler, leader of the National Socialist Party and Chancellor of the new German nation, the Third Reich, which was intended to last for a thousand years. Hitler, who returned the Spear to Germany where it was kept in Nuremberg, used the powers of the Holy Lance deliberately to create a 'master race' which would subjugate the peoples of the world. Adolf Hitler believed that the twentieth century would become a critical turning point in time for the whole evolution of mankind. He imagined that a re-emergence of magical powers would take place with astonishing suddenness. 'The intellect has grown autocratic and become a disease of life. We are at the outset of a tremendous revolution in moral ideas and man's spiritual orientation. A new age of the magic interpretation of the world is coming, an interpretation in terms of the will of the élite and not of intelligence.' To accomplish this Hitler founded the hierarchical order of the SS who were bound together by secret blood rites, the leaders of the *Herrenvolk* who were responsible for carrying out the deliberate policy of genocide – the Holocaust. The Thousand Year Reich, instituted in 1933, came to its bloody and premature end in the ruins of Berlin at the moment the Spear was discovered in Nuremberg, prior to its return to Vienna.

The decision to return the Spear of Destiny to Vienna came directly from General Dwight Eisenhower, the Commander of the Allied Armies in Europe, unwittingly placing the Spear under the rotating protection of the four great powers occupying the capital of Austria. Pending its return to the Hofburg it rested for a short period unceremoniously in the vault of the Austrian Post Office Savings Bank. It was placed there by the embarrassed *Bürgermeister* as a temporary expedient and neither he nor General Mark Clark, who officially handed it over, saw any significance in its arrival in the ancient city now under the stresses of the four-power occupation in an atmosphere of armed antagonism and distrust.

The presence of Britain and France had little significance compared with the mammoth superpowers – America and Russia. The old order of the power of the blood of peoples was over and the apocalyptic era of confrontation between conflicting ideologies had begun and became immediately manifest in the battle for control of the city wherein lay the Spear of Destiny. By the time the Spear had been restored to the Treasure House in the Hofburg, the Iron Curtain had descended and divided Europe into two hostile camps – the exception being the one non-aligned nation, the small neutral state of Austria, the repository of the Holy Lance. It was across the body of this small nation that the two

29

superpowers growled alarmingly at each other like two emerging apocalyptic beasts. Each perceived that for some magical reason they had both been denied control of this seemingly insignificant State and that within it lay the ultimate Destiny of Europe. Thus the apparent parity of strength of the two antagonistic ideologies was given a geographical dimension, delineated by the 'Iron Curtain' and maintained by the so-called principle of deterrence. The age of the balance of terror in the shadow of the Pale Horse had begun and man stood at the threshold where the two apocalyptic faces of evil were revealed.

According to the Book of Job the two Beasts appear at the threshold where the ways of men cease and the ways of God begin – giving man the choice between a change in spiritual and moral attitudes or destruction. The Leviathan who inhabited Hitler and sustained the Nazi regime had been joined by Behemoth the Two-Horned Beast predicted by the Pale Rider whose name is Death and who is followed by the Hosts of Hell.

> And power was given unto them over the fourth part of the earth, to kill with sword, and with hunger, and with death, and with the beasts of the earth.
>
> *Ibid.*, verse 8

30

CHAPTER FOUR

THE SPEAR AND THE TWO FACES OF EVIL

'If thou beest he – but oh, how fallen! how changed
From him! – who in the happy realms of light
Clothed with transcendent brightness, didst outshine
Myriads, though bright! ...'
The Fall of Satan, *Paradise Lost*, Book 1: John Milton

Mankind was stunned at the end of the Second World War when the appalling reality of the genocide that had taken place under the Nazi regime was revealed. Few people were equipped, intellectually or spiritually, to understand the deliberate invocation of demonic powers that had been necessary to carry through the 'final solution'. Not only was this unpalatable truth hidden from public gaze by the smokescreen of the Nuremberg Trials, but it was further obscured by the apocalyptic events at Hiroshima and Nagasaki. Mankind was in reality impelled with such force into the apocalyptic age that we were all thrown unwittingly and involuntarily against the threshold of the spiritual world in which so few believe. This is the threshold where mankind is inevitably confronted by the dual face of evil. The demonic powers lurking on either side of this gateway to higher consciousness can now clearly be seen.

All genuine spiritual experience begins at this threshold and this is why an insight into the twofold face of evil is imperative in our time. The Revelation of St John not only indicates this but tells us how to confront the double evil in a series of powerful imaginations.

31

The twofold Beast of the Revelation is another piece of ancient mythology reborn. Greek mythology also knew the double face of evil. It describes the journeys of Odysseus as the wanderings of the human soul, and shows us how ultimately the hero must find his way between Scylla and Charybdis. He must face the dangers of the shattering rocks as well as the treacherous maelstrom. But Scylla and Charybdis are not merely cliffs and whirlpools; they are supersensible hostile powers which avail themselves of external dangers to destroy the traveller.

How, you may ask, can evil have two faces? Surely there is only one God in heaven while the Devil is in hell? This outdated conception, which belongs to traditional Christian theology, is misleading. The idea of a single force of evil took a strong foothold in medieval Christianity and later is even found in Goethe's *Faust* where the two evils are blended into one in the form of Mephistopheles. The task of mankind in the second half of the twentieth century is to dissect the figure of Mephistopheles and to discover the two separate evils within it and their special ways of working. Even in the mythological symbolism of the Apocalypse, evil is at first concentrated in the figure of a single dragon. However, when the dragon is cast down into the abyss it arises anew in the form of two separate beasts. The 'Dual Face of Evil', described in powerful imaginations in the pages of the Revelation, is relevant to our century and any sensitive human being can now experience how he is tempted from two sides – emotionally from within and from without by physical forces he can neither fully understand nor control. For the mass of humanity, scientists have opened a Pandora's box to release horrors that threaten the very existence of mankind.

The western mind, grounded in materialism, finds the conception of an active force of evil to be totally irrational. The English, like Shakespeare's Hamlet, will not credit a spiritual reality other than a vague belief in the existence of ghosts. The Germanic soul however is different because it is steeped in allusions to the spiritual relationships between heaven and earth which rest at the heart of Teutonic mythology and early German literature where we meet the dual face of evil in the symbolism of the Midgard Snake and the Feneris Wolf at the gates of Valhalla.

The same distinction is implied in the New Testament in which two evil spirits are called by different names. The power, which in the Apocalypse comes out of the sea, is in the Gospels named Diabolos, the Devil who tempts Christ to become Lord of this world; the Beast that rises from dry land is called Satan, the cold calculating spirit who tells Christ to turn stones into bread.

It is only a reference appropriate to modern times when we call the two evil spirits associated with the Spear Lucifer and Ahriman, the names they bore in ancient Persia where the twofold face of evil was first perceived. This is also in agreement with the pictorial wisdom of the Revelation: the seven-headed, ten-horned beast is the Luciferic power; the two-horned beast, the Ahrimanic. And from this pictorial detail in the Revelation we learn that the Luciferic danger threatens us inwardly from the sea of emotions, that is the beast who comes out of the ocean; the Ahrimanic danger threatens us from the environment of earthly life, the beast that arises from dry land. The relationship then is this: the temptation of the hot Luciferic demonry assails man in his inward personal life, whereas the cold Ahrimanic corruption operates more in the form of a social evil in the impersonal relationships of civilization.

The prophecy in the Revelation that the dragon originally seen furled across the sky would reappear in the form of two beasts, was fulfilled when Hitler invoked the powers of the Holy Lance and the single figure of Leviathan rose up to possess him. Behemoth, on the other hand, only became manifest for all eyes to behold when the USA conceived and engineered the atom bomb.

These very same aspects of evil appear in the Old Testament at the point when Job withstands all his trials and sufferings and reaches the portal of the spiritual world. Here he is told: 'Behold now Behemoth ... His bones are tubes of bronze, his limbs like bars of iron' (Job: 40, verses 15, 18, New International Version). The two-horned beast is described as a kind of cold demonic machine, a form which crushes and mangles all creation with its claws and teeth. Then Job is asked, 'Knowest thou Leviathan?' Job now sees a beast living in the passions of vanity, ambition, pride and lust for power. The danger of this beast is that he denies all morality and spiritual aims. Leviathan is presented as a figure of soul without spirit; Behemoth is spirit without soul.

Of course in religious mythology Lucifer is responsible for the fall of mankind from paradise. Restated in the terminology of the evolution of consciousness Lucifer brings self-conscious thinking to man and in so doing divides him from his natural spiritual inheritance. It is at this point that the Ahrimanic powers step in to persuade man that there is only one reality – the reality of the sense world out of which the whole universe can be explained in scientific terms. Ahriman has to a large extent removed the influence of Lucifer from many aspects of the modern scene. The Ahrimanic forces dominate the world today. Ahriman, the lord of the physical world, is the very spirit of modern technology. He works in the cold, soulless, machine-driven intellectual climate of our impersonal mechanized age. It is also Ahriman who directs the sense-derived consciousness of scientific materialism and cold computer calculation which ultimately reduces man himself to an impersonal statistical cypher. No sane person would wish to reverse industrial progress but we must learn to use this

Ahrimanically inspired technology so that we do not become slaves to it.

The Revelation clearly reveals that the Ahrimanic powers will hypnotize mankind into accepting the phenomenal world as the whole world, creating the illusion of materialism. Under such an illusion the conscience of men can be undermined leading to a state of moral degeneration in which human life is so undervalued that man himself becomes totally subservient to the ideology that rules him. In this milieu the ideologies of both left and right will develop until the State has total control not only over the individual but also over the way in which he thinks. This amoral condition insidiously created by Ahriman leaves mankind totally vulnerable to the Luciferic powers awaiting humanity as their prey. This is why the Revelation informs us that the second beast does not itself come fully into sight but remains in the background in order to betray mankind to the first beast. It does not take much imagination to see that this is the condition in which humanity finds itself today.

This hidden alliance between the two faces of evil continually manifests itself in new forms and comes to expression in the fusion of science and industry that first clearly emerged during the Second World War and now has its most far-reaching effects in the marriage between atomic physics and aeronautical engineering.

Towards the end of the Second World War the Luciferically inspired triumph of a new scientific aristocracy was unleashed in the form of a nuclear fireball. Fortunately in this new and horrendous field of endeavour the two separate and contrasting powers of evil were not yet able to join hands because the Ahrimanically inspired engineers who were developing rocket weapons were members of the German proletariat involved in a last, frantic but belated effort to save Hitler's Third Reich. The combination of the

Luciferic thinking of pure science and the actions of the Ahrimanic engineers only took place with devastating effect in the aftermath of the European Holocaust when Russia had also become a nuclear power and vied with the Americans in the search for German rocket technicians to build the missiles which created 'the balance of terror'. It is this unholy alliance which the Revelation characterizes as the 'Age of the Pale Horse' in which the 'Hosts of Hell' can unleash an ever-increasing number of new means with which to threaten mankind with annihilation. An ideological fissure now emerged which reached across the globe and permeated into every realm of human activity. This was the international situation in which the Iron Curtain descended to divide Europe into opposing camps and reflect the worldwide conflict between the new ideologies.

Hidden within the contrasting ideologies of East and West the same two powers of evil are masquerading in a cunning alliance which creates the apparent differences between western Capitalism and eastern Communism. Despite these apparent differences the two ideologies are in reality different manifestations of the same demonic theme – the creation of a new ruling aristocracy based not on blood and heredity, but solely on the power of money in the West, and on a naked bureaucracy of power based on the Party élite in the East. Both use the most modern aspects of computerized technology to maintain and extend their hold on their peoples. The ability of these élites to maintain power is contrived in the West by the use of Ahrimanic means to control the masses who live under the Luciferic illusion that material gratification is freedom; and in the East by a Luciferic bureaucracy under the guise of the Ahrimanic and illusionary ideal of equality of opportunity for all. The two ideologies which have brought mankind to the brink of extermination are simply mirror images of each other showing a classical form of lateral inversion that masks their true nature.

The United Nations merely provides the stage on which the two mammoth superpowers publicly display their hostility and at the same time attempt to win over allies from the newer nations who gained their freedom from the declining empires of Britain, France and Holland. Was the election of Kurt Waldheim as General Secretary of the United Nations yet another machination of the twofold face of evil? Or was it the result of collusion between two hostile superpowers where each sought to gain a separate advantage on the negotiating tables of the UN? The only other possibility could be that Kurt Waldheim himself had immediate personal recourse to powers of another kind! Why did this ageing man later cling so obstinately to the position of President of the small and seemingly unimportant nation of Austria even when subjected to painful and sustained harassment by the world's press for his part in genocide?

The present claimant to the Spear of Destiny is no longer a member of a hereditary ruling class, but the incumbent President of Austria!

SECTION 2

THE HEART OF THE MATTER

The Pathway to Spiritual Perception and the Meaning of Personal Destiny in Our Time

Thank God our time is now
When wrong comes up to meet us everywhere
Never to leave us till we take
The greatest stride of soul
Men ever took.
Affairs are now soul size
The enterprise
Is Exploration unto God.
Where are you making for?
It takes so many thousand years to wake.
But will you wake
For pity's sake?

A Sleep of Prisoners: Christopher Fry

Two separate streams have run parallel to one another throughout history. One stream has always been outwardly visible; the other has been hidden to all eyes but those of the initiated. Only the first stream has been commonly known as 'history' but hidden behind it at all times was the other stream which continually guided it and shaped it further. This situation is changing today because mankind as a whole stands at the threshold of the spiritual world and can awaken to the path of initiation which is now open to everybody and not restricted, as previously, to the select few.

The Spear of Destiny is a resonator of the same spiritual

faculties with which St John perceived the spiritual world and wrote the Revelation. And it is with these faculties that we can begin to interpret the strange mythological symbolism of St John and relate it to the unfolding script of history in our time; they have an indispensable function in revealing the spiritual background behind contemporary events and in distinguishing the workings of good and evil powers.

These very faculties, which so urgently need to come to birth in all mankind, were used to discover an apocalyptic calendar in stone, the hidden configuration built by the Chartres Masters, which accurately dates the critical phase of the Apocalypse at the end of this century.

The rituals and techniques of initiation of the ancient craftmasons who built the great cathedrals of the Middle Ages anticipated the re-emergence of their own spiritual faculties in the twentieth century as a natural inheritance for all mankind. Craftmasonry itself came to an abrupt end in the beginning of the eighteenth century to be replaced by Freemasonry which tragically developed both an enlightened and a sinister stream. The enlightened stream inspired the writing of the American Constitution while the black adepts misused their occult knowledge for financial and political gain.

The new spiritual insight gained at the threshold of the spiritual world leads along a path of self knowledge to the unveiling of the meaning of personal destiny through which the process of reincarnation from life to life is revealed. The next consecutive step in the spiritual progress of humanity is an understanding of the relationship between personal destiny and the progress of world history.

The Revelation of St John presupposes that the drama and symbolism of history is the result of the interweaving of reincarnation patterns. The nail held by three metal threads within the blade of the Spear of Longinus represents individual destiny and its place in the ongoing history of mankind. Examples of the sequence of former reincarnations of great historical personalities demonstrate how the passage of history is indeed a very personal affair for all of us.

CHAPTER FIVE

THE SPEAR AS RESONATOR OF SPIRITUAL FACULTIES

The Spear of Destiny was a talisman of Spiritual Power from the time it was first forged by Phineas as a magical symbol of the blood of the Chosen People. It became charged as the most important resonator of spiritual faculties in the singular mighty ritual of the crucifixion at Golgotha when it pierced the side of Christ, releasing the flow of the blood which brought about the birth of the cosmic Christ as the earth spirit. At that instant the veil of the 'Holy of Holies' in the Temple was rent to expose the black cube of the Old Covenant which now split along its sides to open out into the form of the cross. The Spear working as a catalyst of Revelation ended the imageless cult of Jehovah. The veiled mystery of the Old Covenant had lost its validity and power, to give place to the beginning of a new vista in the destiny of humanity which opened the heavens to all mankind. It was out of this new vista that an old hermit, living in a cave in the penal island of Patmos, wrote the Revelation, opening the doors of perception in a new form of Christian initiation – the Christianity of the Holy Grail.

St John transcended the barriers of time to reveal the spiritual background to a vast panorama of the past and future history of humanity. Our problem today is how to decipher the symbolism in which he recorded these events so that his Revelation becomes for us a kind of magic mirror through which we can see the hand of the Apocalypse

42

within the fabric of unfolding events. For what sense can the rational mind of today make of this mysterious work which clothes the destiny of mankind in a framework of Seals, Trumpet Blasts and Vials of Wrath?

The enigmas arising from pictorial symbolism of a bygone age are compounded by the radical changes in consciousness that have taken place in the last two thousand years. It is precisely these changes in consciousness, the very substance and the mainspring of history, that have been overlooked by archeologists and historians. Modern researchers think of early man as originally possessing no more than an awareness of his physical surroundings, and then gradually expanding this awareness and extending his intellectual activities. Yet the Revelation seems to suggest that the direction of the historical process is exactly the reverse in a process that can only be called a contraction of consciousness. And it is just such a reversal which makes the enigma of St John's four horsemen comprehensible.

However strange it might appear to the modern mind the evidence seems to indicate that man was originally so close to the spiritual world that he was more aware of divine beings or gods than he was of objects presented in the terrestrial world around him. It seems that he apprehended these beings in pictures, very much as dim perceptions and memories form themselves today into pictures in a dream. For instance, when ancient man looked up to the stars it appears that he did not see the individual points of light in the sky which present themselves to our senses today. Instead, the starry structures in space lit up pictures in his mind – such pictures as the craftmasons later carved in stone on the portals of the great cathedrals of Europe in the Middle Ages to represent the mythological constellations of the zodiac which are regarded by most people today as no more than ingenious fantasy.

Such an alternative view of the early consciousness of

man, suggested in the imagery of the Revelation, is in harmony with the ancient traditions of all peoples who invariably speak of a divine origin for their practical skills. Zarathustra learns the art of agriculture from the sun god, Ahura Mazdā; Osiris teaches the Egyptians the art of growing corn; Dionysus travels the lands imparting the knowledge of the vine; Moses receives the Table of the Law from Jehovah on Mount Sinai; Khammurabi is personally instructed by the god Shamash; Numa Pompilius is inspired to instigate the religious rituals of Rome by the goddess Egeria in a sacred grove. All early handicrafts are also connected with religious cults.

The first concrete evidence of the nature of ancient consciousness appears around the year 3000 BC with the earliest writings of mankind in stone, tablets of clay and on papyrus in the form of hieroglyphics and cuneiform. But because of the very strangeness of the historical context a great deal of guesswork is involved in the interpretation and most modern scholars project into it their own subjectivity without any awareness of the importance of the distortions they make.

The first writing in human history in which we have any certainty of translation is the *Iliad*, the events of which took place around 1230 BC and were written down some three hundred years later. A very significant and revealing picture of the mind of the *Iliad* has arisen from researches into *The Origin of Consciousness* by Julian Jaynes, an American psychologist. Jaynes insists that there is absolutely no indication of self-consciousness in the pages of the *Iliad* and, speaking generally, no signs of any consciousness at all in this epic. That is to say Jaynes can find no words in it which denote consciousness or mental acts of any sort. He sees the characters of the *Iliad* as noble automata who were totally unconscious of themselves, their emotions, their acts and even of their own bodies. What he describes seems somewhat reminiscent of the fairytale figure 'Pinocchio' before he awakened to himself and his surroundings and wished to become human!

This is the condition of mankind depicted in symbolism of the age of the White Horse which would be gradually replaced during the next thousand years by the self-conscious thinking of the Greco–Latin age – the age of the Red Horse in which St John the Divine wrote the Revelation.

The new spiritual faculties which St John was the first to gain as a result of his Christian initiation are depicted in the Revelation as Seals, Trumpet Blasts and Vials of Wrath. These are the very same faculties that an individual must develop today when humanity has become ripe enough to use a re-emerging supersensible perception through which the unfolding events of the Apocalypse will become meaningful.

The Seals represent a kind of *Imaginative Cognition* which clothes the spiritual reality in an extension of physical seeing – a seeing with the eye of the mind. Such a magical power of transformed thinking expresses itself in vivid images and pictures which the prophetic apostle himself uses in the Revelation. This new kind of vision reveals not only the spiritual realities and processes at work within man's own being but also behind the physical world of nature.

The Trumpet Blasts symbolize the faculty of *Inspiration* which is an extension of physical hearing involving man's whole being. This faculty of direct spiritual hearing is born when an individual gains the power to empty his consciousness not only of all sense impressions but also the vivid picture imagery gained by the newly acquired faculty of imaginative cognition. And within such an emptied consciousness a higher world of spiritual beings and supersensible happenings arises. The very word Inspiration

45

presupposes the flowing of the spirit world into an emptied consciousness in the same manner as air is inhaled into the physical lungs. A world of celestial beings is now revealed and their nature and activity is expressed in the endless and varying relationships in which they stand to one another. The active interweaving of these celestial hierarchies is deciphered by Inspiration like the reading of a script. Thus the strange and apparently unworldly symbolism used in the Revelation is transformed into a meaningful reality.

Just as imagination involves the transformation of normal everyday consciousness, and Inspiration delves into the realm of the subconsciousness, so *Intuition*, symbolized by the Vials of Wrath, brings light into the arena of the collective unconsciousness. Intuition unveils the individual human spirit and how it belongs within the spiritual world. And this leads beyond the mere perception of spiritual beings, bringing the resolution and ability to enter into direct and conscious relationship with them. In order to develop such intuition a self-discipline of the highest order is needed, especially the annihilation of personal egoism and the development of a pure disinterested love of others. Through Intuition a person not only becomes aware of the nature of his own existence as an eternal spirit but also gains a direct inner knowing of the very nature and motives of the ascending grades of beings who inhabit the spiritual world.

It is the very succession of these unlikely symbols in the form of Seals, Trumpet Blasts and Vials of Wrath, along with the Four Horses of the Apocalypse, that creates the whole temporal structure of the Revelation, relating the celestial imagery to the events in the historical process. These events described in mysterious imagery can only take place at this moment in history when mankind is now once again capable of developing those faculties through which the significant happenings can be meaningfully understood.

We need not be very acute observers of the changing scenes of our own times to notice how great masses of people today are unconsciously demonstrating an urgent need to experience these three spiritual faculties – Imagination, Inspiration and Intuition.

A massive inner urge towards the picture consciousness of spiritual vision has been outwardly replaced by an insatiable desire for coloured illustrations in comics and illustrated newspapers and magazines. While more sophisticated substitutes such as films, television and video actually kill off the budding imaginative picture faculty which seeks to come to birth.

Inspiration, which presupposes an inner faculty of hearing, seeks with equal insistence to come to fruition but under the pressures of modern civilization few people any longer know how to listen. Their souls have become deaf to the real sound behind nature and music. This urgent inner need of the human soul has been outwardly satisfied by the emergence of 'pop music' which pours forth ceaselessly from radio channels across the globe to quash the budding faculty of inspired hearing.

The inner longing for intuition, which exists with such intensity in the isolated consciousness of humanity today, has founded substitutes which have created chaos in the destiny of mankind. Intuition, a faculty born of the highest form of human love, seeks to become one in spirit with everything which the soul beholds. False fulfilments, which replace the real longing for love, are now apparent in all too prevalent promiscuity. Erotic fantasy, projected everywhere for commercial gain, finds its completion without conscience in an instinctive but loveless sexuality.

The new spiritual senses and spiritual faculties which were first developed in the Christian initiation of St John out of which he wrote the Revelation, must now be developed by humanity in the present age. The new path of

Christian initiation seeks to overcome the materialistic entrapment which is known allegorically in the Bible as 'The Fall from Paradise'. The Spear in this context actually represents the fate of mankind because it pierced the side of Christ in the redemptive ritual of Golgotha. When the Roman Centurion Longinus wielded the Spear he was the instrument of the very fate from which Christ had come to free mankind. The flow to the earth of the redemptive blood of the Saviour reopened the gates of spiritual perception to all mankind. Sadly, at first, such perception could only be the preserve of a hidden thread of initiates who kept the knowledge alive through the ensuing centuries. It is only now that humanity is spiritually ripe enough to develop and use these faculties once more.

At the present time when the apocalyptic events of the twentieth century hurl humanity against the threshold of the spiritual world, each individual must make a choice between a good and an evil path – a choice which depends on his or her understanding of personal destiny. This is why 'The Holy Lance' assumes such a singular importance at this time because it holds the key to the meaning of personal destiny.

Three separate factors are at work in the outer events and inner development in the life of each individual: fate, freedom and grace. But, in order to show exactly how these three factors work in the unfolding of personal destiny, we must first learn something about the origin of the concept of fate, or karma, and the laws which govern its working.

Behind the allegory of the expulsion of Adam and Eve from Paradise which is described in Genesis, are three inescapable facts of life which confront all mankind: *toil, pain* and *death*. Pain in every birth, toil to survive in the face of hostile nature, death to all created beings. This conception is not unique to the Old Testament; it is the foundation of far older religious systems in which it was called '*primal karma*'. It is this primal karma which underlies the meaning of personal destiny which by necessity arises out of it.

Only two basic attitudes are possible towards this fate of mankind. It can be regarded as a curse that has arisen from a blind evolution or it can be regarded as a purposeful blessing at the hand of God. The original path of initiation arose from the latter view in which toil, pain and death were regarded as the means through which humanity was protected from evil.

The first known system of initiation appeared in ancient Persia around 7000 BC when Zarathustra divined the conversion of these three primal necessities. Through the spiritualization of toil, meditation arose; through the voluntary acceptance of pain, the mystery trials of initiation were created; through the spiritualization of death, initiation into the spiritual worlds arose. Through meditation the organs of spiritual vision were developed; mystery trials were devised to prepare for existence in the spiritual world; while the body lay as dead in a three-day temple sleep, the soul was guided into the spiritual world itself.

The ancient initiates who were inhabitants of two worlds, the terrestrial and the supersensible, guided their peoples as priest-kings, of which the ancient Pharaohs are the best known examples. But such initiates existed amongst all peoples in many guises; for instance, Moses, Phineas and Elijah in the Old Testament, Numa Pompilius and Vergil in Rome, and Plato, Socrates and Aristotle in Athens. By the time of the birth of Christ, the mystery temples were in complete decline and the gateway of spiritual initiation was closed until it was reopened by the sacrificial ritual at Golgotha which took place publicly on the open arena of history for all mankind to see, thus revealing for the first time the hidden secrets of initiation.

One of the major contributory factors that led the Sanhedrin to the decision to kill Christ was that in his teachings and in his actions, raising Lazarus from the dead for instance, he had made public the hidden mysteries of initiation. The penalty for revealing these hidden mysteries had always been death and this is why St John wrote his Revelation in a mystical symbolism which could not be deciphered by the uneducated masses.

After the advent of Christianity, the first person of real influence to teach these secrets openly, was Mani who lived in the third century in the Middle East. Mani, an orphan child, worked as a slave in the home of a sage in Baghdad who traded in art treasures and antiquities, and who kept an archive of the initiation cults of ancient civilizations. After the death of his master, Mani was discovered by his widow studying these ancient documents. She adopted him, paid for his education and encouraged his studies. He was further encouraged, from beyond the grave, by his late master.

He grew up to become the founder of one of the most profound mystical and philosophical systems of the world – a Christian initiation cult through which the human soul could not only achieve spiritual perception but also ascend through seven prescribed degrees to a full participation in the spiritual world.

Mani taught publicly in a truly imaginative way of the battle in the universe between light and darkness, good and evil. Above all he gave a truly moral conception of the overcoming of evil not by conflict but by love and passive resistance. The core of his teaching was the conception that mankind was created in order to transform the evil in the universe to the power of love. He was the first Christian initiate to include the teaching of reincarnation as a way in which the sins of man could be made good again in a subsequent earthly life. He was condemned to death for divulging the secrets of initiation and preaching a religious message that directly contradicted the teachings of the

Magi in the kingdom of Shapur. His terrible fate was to be skinned alive.

The initiation cult of the Manichees spread into eastern Europe and then to France where it met with terrible persecution, especially the Cathar communities living around Toulouse in the thirteenth century who were burned or put to the sword with savage brutality.

The Manichaean stream most closely associated with the Spear of Destiny was linked to the family who possessed it in the ninth century when the search for the Grail itself became a path of initiation. Around the characters who sought the Grail in that century the epic of *Parzival* was written some eleven generations later by the wandering minnesinger Wolfram von Eschenbach, who reveals within this saga the symbolism of the seven degrees of initiation. The raven was the sign of the first degree because it symbolized the messenger of the gods. The peacock signified the second degree, its many-splendoured plumage demonstrating the capacity for powers of moral imagination. The knight became the symbol of the third and warrior degree and knighthood was bestowed for the attainment of it. The swan was the sign of the fourth degree not only because of its purity but also because the swansong represented the death of self and the inner realization of the divine within the human breast.

The fifth degree in the Grail symbolism was depicted by the pelican, the bird which wounds its own breast to feed its young; such an initiate lived for the perpetuation of his own people and dedicated his life to their service. The eagle denoted the sixth degree in which an initiate gained the capacity to move and communicate in the spiritual world. The crown was the symbol of the King of the Grail who had achieved the very highest degree. To him was revealed the secrets of time and an understanding of the laws at work within human destiny.

51

The Grail initiation continued in secret until the formation of the Templars in Jerusalem in 1119 AD after the first crusade. Ostensibly the Templars were founded with papal blessing to protect pilgrims to the Holy Land but the real reason is hidden in history. The first Knights Templar were quartered in the former stables of King Solomon beside the site of the destroyed Temple. It was here that the Ark of the Covenant had been hidden from the Roman soldiers of Trajan. Hugo de Payne, a close friend and relative of Chretien le Troyes, had been chosen to unearth the Ark and to bring it back to Europe where it was later hidden beneath the crypt of Chartres Cathedral.

The warrior monks of the Knights Templar were bound by vows of poverty and chastity, like many similar Orders. The difference between them and other Orders was that they were also initiates who were bound to secrecy on pain of death if they revealed the hidden path they followed. Within a hundred years they were the richest and most powerful Order in Europe, more powerful than any single kingdom and rivalling in power the Church of Rome itself. Unlike the Church they did not concern themselves with the salvation of individual souls, but with the transformation of the lives of whole communities and nations to create a new European Christendom. Above all they became a threat to the power of kings and to the feudal structure of Europe. At the same time they were revered by the common people because they had freed the roads of Europe from the brigandage of the local barons. All this was achieved in association with the powers of the Spear which now outwardly became part of their insignia.

Although their integrity and unselfishness had gained wide respect, the independence and wealth of the Order aroused the envy of the Church and King Philip the Fair of France. Hiding from the wrath of his people King Philip took refuge with the Order and discovered in the temple where he sheltered vast hoards of gold. For personal greed he began to plan the destruction of the Knights Templar and make the wealth of the Order his own.

King Philip, acting in collusion with Pope Clement, invited the leaders of the Order to a banquet at his palace. The unarmed and unsuspecting Grand Master, Jacques de Molay, together with his élite were arrested on charges of heresy and idolatry. At the same time the leaders of the Order in other European cities were also arrested and imprisoned. Over a period of five years the Templar Knights were subjected to terrible torture in an attempt to make them confess to black magic practices of which they were entirely innocent. Finally Jacques de Molay, hoping to alleviate the suffering of his brothers, confessed to the worship of Baphomet. On the stake he recanted and prophesied the deaths of King Philip, the Pope and the Chief Inquisitor as a punishment for their conspiracy. Within the appointed time all three died and the curse they themselves had laid on the Royal House lasted until the beheading of the last Bourbon King on the same spot during the French Revolution.

Within the enclosing spiritual darkness of the final centuries of the Middle Ages, a new path of initiation arose out of the impulse of Christian Rosenkreuz, one of the greatest initiates in the history of Christendom. The Rosicrucians, a hidden stream of initiation, who worked completely unnoticed by the Inquisition, used their spiritual faculties to inspire the craftmasons who built the great cathedrals of Europe.

CHAPTER SIX

PROPHETIC PILLARS OF THE APOCALYPSE

There is a great unsolved mystery regarding the sudden outburst of cathedral building in Europe in the Middle Ages which has no parallel anywhere in the entire history of architecture. In this regard a new and significant question arises: did an alignment of some of these specially sited and uniquely constructed cathedrals hide a secret configuration to represent the earth as the Temple of God?

The puzzling murder of an apprentice by a master mason in the fifteenth century aroused the interest of a scholar in the twentieth century. The manner in which this murder was committed led to the discovery of an intriguing alignment of some of the great cathedrals. Using the spiritual faculties already described he discovered that this alignment forms a monumental predictive calendar which accurately dates the critical turning point of the Apocalypse to take place in the year two thousand.

The mass of humanity had lost the last vestiges of spiritual awareness by the middle of the fifteenth century, the beginning of the epoch of the Black Horse which symbolizes the commencement of the materialistic age. It is not difficult to see why the fifteenth century marks a critical turning point in the history of western thought. This was the century which ushered out the Middle Ages and witnessed the dawn of the Renaissance which served to further a deepening interest in unveiling the secrets of the physical world and harnessing its forces for material ends.

Suddenly a flat, unmoving earth, supposedly the very centre of the universe, became a planet among planets revolving around the sun in accordance with natural laws. Galileo would soon invent the thermometer and instigate the 'pointer reading' age. His conviction that mathematical concepts could be applied to natural events swept theology from its central position in European thought and began to replace it with systems of mathematical logic. The ancient paradigm of 'Heaven, Earth and Hell', so sublimely epitomized in the work of Dante was about to be replaced by the new world conception of Copernicus with its dynamic and heliocentric description of the solar system. Together with Kepler's laws, it would create a pathway for Newtonian physics. The sublime description of creation in Genesis would give way to Darwin's *The Origin of Species*. Mankind stood on the brink of the 'Age of Discovery' through which a new world would be discovered and man would begin to familiarize himself with the dimensions and the geography of the planet. The Royal Society would soon be founded in England, and Francis Bacon would appear as the father of modern scientific method, insisting that the world of the senses alone can provide us with realities, the realities of the empirical method.

The new age of inductive reasoning was under way and man became very quickly at home with the forces of the physical world. Yet the discovery of the earth, the investigation of the properties of matter, the promulgation of new laws at work in the universe, the invention of machines and new sources of power to drive them, the new views of space and time − all these are not signs of a greater acuteness or penetration of mind but rather the result of mind itself moving into a new sphere. Somehow consciousness had entered the realm of the mechanical forces of the earth in which yet more triumphs of invention and technique awaited it.

55

Since there was no apparent physiological reason that might explain this sudden change in man's capacities for thought, and none were sought by the mainstream historians, the true reason for this sudden dramatic change in human consciousness remained hidden until the middle of this century. When researching *The Spear of Destiny* this enigma puzzled and fascinated Trevor Ravenscroft who discovered the answer by chance through a stone carving completed by the craftmasons in the middle of the fifteenth century. The carving was a piece of dramatic symbolism that depicted this very change when man was finally severed from all perception of the spiritual world and isolated in a purely material existence.

This moment of historical illumination took place in an ancient but little-known church in Roslin near Edinburgh in Scotland when he discovered a carving of a human head with a gaping wound in the right temple. No extant historical record but only a somewhat garbled legend explained the presence on consecrated ground of this stone head with a naked gash carved into the right frontal lobe of the brain. The legend, passed down by word of mouth over the centuries, tells of the murder of an apprentice by a master mason at the time the church, originally intended to have been a great cathedral, was started in 1449.

The master mason having received from his patron the model of a pillar of exquisite workmanship and design, hesitated to carry it out until he had been to Rome or some such foreign part, and seen the original. He went abroad, and in his absence an apprentice, having dreamed the finished pillar, at once set to work and carried out the design as it now stands, a perfect marvel of workmanship. The master mason on his return was so stung with envy that he asked who had dared to do it in his absence. On being told it was his own apprentice, he was so inflamed with rage and passion that he struck him with his mallet, killed him on the spot, and paid the penalty for his rash and cruel act.

Rosslyn Chapel Guidebook

If this legend is true, the head of the apprentice with the wound in his right cerebral hemisphere has been looking down on the pillar of his own creation for some five hundred years. The pillar on which his sightless eyes are directed, known today as 'the prentice pillar', is carved to represent the Tree of Life. The pillar has a uniqueness of design and quality of workmanship surpassing the rest of the superb carving in this building which was originally to have been the east wing of a great Roman Catholic cathedral built in the form of a cross. When Ravenscroft made his first visit to Roslin some twenty-eight years ago and saw the carved head of the apprentice with the wounded brain he knew immediately that he beheld the dramatic symbolism which depicted the most significant change in the very nature of human consciousness, the moment when western man finally became severed from all perception of his spiritual origin and isolated in a purely materialistic existence.

He was awed at the very profundity of the mystery he was confronting. And yet, it was at the same instant that he asked himself what might at first appear to be a totally irrational question: 'Would the head of the apprentice have been carved at all, and would the legend have survived into modern times, if the death blow had been struck into the left temple?' With spiritual insight he came to the conclusion that there would have been neither carving nor legend if the lethal stroke had not cut into the right frontal lobe!

Although he reached this apparently bizarre conclusion in a flash of intuition, his intuition was later confirmed by an intensive and prolonged study of the world conception and the initiation rituals of the craftmasons – and especially through an insight into their unique knowledge of the different modes of working of the two distinct and separate hemispheres of the human brain.

This moment of insight was later reinforced by the modern scientific discovery of these two different modes of operation of the left and right hemispheres which first emerged some six years later as a working hypothesis from the cumulative results of a century of neuro-surgery and psychological research into brain lesions and the consequent localizing of the many and complex mental activities to specific areas of the brain.

A new dichotomy has arisen which has been so widely publicized and is generally known that we need only recapitulate it very briefly here. The two modes of consciousness in this dichotomy are classified today:

The left hemisphere (controlling the right side of the body) is spoken of as 'masculine, profane, active, intellectual, analytical, linear, sequential and causal.'

The right hemisphere (associated with the left side of the body) is considered to be 'feminine, sacred, receptive, intuitive, holistic, non-linear, simultaneous, spatial and acausal.' And, of course, contemporary human consciousness is regarded as an integration of both modes, each occupation or discipline involving the dominance of some aspect of one or the other. In fact the two vital aspects of this dichotomy are that the reflection into consciousness of the *Senses of the Body* which serve the intellect, take place in the left lobe; while the *Senses of the Spirit* which serve the soul, occur in the right.

The craftmasons of the Middle Ages were aware of supersensible realities to which the physical senses are blind. In this manner they were able to perceive the spiritual background of physical existence. In this respect they regarded the right hemisphere of the brain as a counterpart of the left hemisphere with which man reflects with intellectual faculties upon the three-dimensional world in which he lives. For they conceived the right hemisphere as the framework for the spiritual faculties through which man orientates himself within the higher dimensions of the spiritual world visible to the senses of the spirit. If the masters of craftmasonry who built the great cathedrals of Europe were alive today, they would show no astonishment at the public discovery of their once secret knowledge regarding the different modes of operation of the two separate and complementary hemispheres. In fact, and we will later illustrate how, they anticipated that this rediscovery would come about after a period of five hundred years.

The initiation rituals of craftmasonry have always included the ritual slaying of an apprentice, purely symbolic of course. In one particular scene of this dramatic mystery symbolism which takes place in the secrecy of the lodge, an apprentice presents a triangular-shaped stone instead of the customary square or oblong stone used in the building work. And for this reason he is judged to be both false and an intruder. He is supposedly put to death by a blow to the right temple delivered with a maul, the cube-shaped gavel of the ritual master. But later, when the brotherhood seek in vain for a specially shaped stone to fit as the keystone of the royal arch, the triangular stone of the apprentice is retrieved from the rubble to assume its true and triumphant place. The apprentice arises from a coffin to become the new grandmaster of the lodge. His triangular stone represents the three spiritual faculties of imaginative cognition, inspiration and intuition which man must reanimate to comprehend the spiritual world.

It is significant in this ritual that the apprentice should be struck in the *right temple* with a cube-shaped gavel. The cube or square is the symbol of the earth-fettered three-dimensional consciousness of the left frontal lobe of the brain. Whereas the wound it causes in the right temple represents

59

the increasing incapacity of the right cerebral hemisphere to work as the vehicle through which the three spiritual faculties of man can unveil the supersensible realities of the spiritual world.

By the middle of the fifteenth century, the beginning of the epoch of the Black Horse, the last vestiges of the ancient clairvoyant vision had atrophied to close the gates to spiritual perception. And at the same time the subtle physiological changes taking place in the right hemisphere over the millennia now reached their culmination and wounded the right frontal lobe to such an extent that it could no longer serve the faculties of the spirit.

It was precisely at this moment of critical change in consciousness around AD 1450 that Rosslyn Chapel was founded. And when the master mason slew his apprentice in a fit of envy, his misguided deed not only fulfilled publicly the dramatic symbolism of an ancient and secret ritual but it also demonstrated unwittingly like an historical synchronism the crucial change in human consciousness which was taking place at this very time in the historical process.

Above the prentice pillar at Rosslyn are carvings of the Seals, Trumpets and Vials clearly demonstrating that the old craftmasons understood not only the symbolism of St John, but also foresaw the reawakening of consciousness in our time that he had foretold. These carvings and other clues in that building led us to the discovery that the craftmasons have also left us a much more vital record, a tangible and monumental form of calendar that dates precisely the critical turning point of the main events of the apocalyptic age in which we live.

How can we be sure exactly when the prophesied events in the Revelation will take place? It was in answer to this question that I began to consider whether the cathedral builders of the Middle Ages had left behind some clues regarding the future date of these formidable events which the Revelation predicts will take place on a planetary scale.

I had the deepest intuition that the wound in the carved head of the apprentice and the pillar on which his sightless eyes looked down provided a vital clue. And, though the answer to this riddle evaded me for a while, I could not put aside the conviction that the actual geographical location of Rosslyn and the prentice pillar was an integral part of some great unsolved mystery concerning both the symbolism of the Apocalypse and the exact date in which its most crucial events would take place. I began to consider the whole tradition of craftmasonry which was based on the building of the original Temple in Jerusalem. It seemed significant that, after the final destruction of the Temple by Trajan in AD 79, the symbolic Temple of the Revelation of St John was considered to represent the 'New Jerusalem', a future age when the source of divine revelation would be restored to mankind, creating a new world order and the establishment of a human civilization in which the powers of evil would find no place.

The cathedral builders of the Middle Ages took a more immediate and practical interest in the description of the New Jerusalem because they saw it in terms of measure and proportion to represent the Earth itself as the Temple of God. 'Rise and measure the Temple of God' says St John. And the cathedral builders did just that. Familiar with the canons of measurement which apply to the figures of sacred geometry, they discovered that the measurements of the New Jerusalem given in Revelation were exactly in proportion to the measurements of the planet Earth on a scale of one foot to one mile.

I had always believed that there was some great unsolved mystery regarding the outburst of cathedral building in Europe in the twelfth and thirteenth centuries which had no parallel in the entire history of architecture. But now in this regard a new and significant question began to frame itself in my mind: 'Did an alignment of some of these specially sited and uniquely constructed cathedrals hide a secret configuration built to represent the earth as the Temple of God as it is described in the Revelation?'

It appeared more than likely that the 'Prentice Pillar' within the uncompleted building in Rosslyn, which was originally planned ás the last of the great cathedrals, was the final piece in this hidden configuration. I became so absorbed in this riddle that I jettisoned my career in London and moved up to live in Scotland. I could not find accommodation in Roslin itself so I rented a cottage some distance away. It was only after I had moved in that I discovered that the ruins beside this cottage were the last remnants of a monastery in which the murdered apprentice who built the pillar had once lived. It was the first of a series of incredible coincidences which accompanied my quest.

For the next two years I spent my spare time studying the architecture of Rosslyn Chapel, exploring its natural surroundings, researching the historical background to the period, deciphering the rich profusion of carvings, and investigating every known facet of the illustrious life of its founder.

Roslin marks the end of the original Great North Road, which was built during the Roman occupation of Britain and which stretches from the Channel coast through the entire length of England to Scotland. Roslin village, far older than Edinburgh and dating back to the second century AD, is shaped like a cross. And when Rosslyn Chapel was built in the fifteenth century, it was placed at the head of this cross. Mellow with age, the Chapel stands on a ridge overlooking the river Esk. At the time of its foundation in 1447, the site stood in the heart of a great forest teeming with deer and wildlife. Today the natural surroundings still retain a deep mystical quality which has attracted innumerable poets to this sacred place across the centuries, including William Wordsworth, Lord Byron and Sir Walter Scott.

At first sight, the Chapel itself appears small, squat and even somewhat grotesque with its lines of buttresses topped by square and conical towers. Even the most inexperienced eye can tell instantly that the building is unfinished. Only the choir has been completed. It stands on thirteen pillars which form an arcade of twelve pointed arches which represent the twelve constellations of the Zodiac. Three further pillars divide the east aisle from the Lady Chapel which extends the whole length of the building. The roof of the choir is barrel vaulted and built in stone. It is powdered in diaper work with a profusion of stars, lilies and roses – medieval symbolism which contains one of the keys to the true significance of Rosslyn as the last piece of a huge configuration representing the Apocalypse in stone.

The original building was intended to be a great sanctuary in the form of a cross with a high tower in the centre. The foundations of the whole building, which were fully laid, were rediscovered at the end of the eighteenth century; the foundations for the huge nave stretching some ninety feet. If the entire plan had been carried out it would have formed a unique and majestic cathedral, completely outshining all other churches in Scotland at this period. What gives Rosslyn Chapel its reputation today as a unique shrine is the variety, candour and exuberance of its endless rich profusion of carvings which have no equal anywhere else in Britain.

The most important question for me at this time concerned the destination of the master mason who went off according to the legend to find the original and complimentary pillar. His journey certainly seemed to confirm the tradition of craftmasonry in which two pillars supported the royal arch above the portal of the original Temple of King

Solomon on Mount Moriah in Jerusalem. These pillars, known as Boaz, the pillar of strength, and Jachin, the pillar of wisdom, are normally found side by side in any masonic temple where they are the two basic symbols of craftmasonry. But in Rosslyn Chapel only Boaz, in this instance the prentice pillar, is present. I sensed that the other pillar would be located at the other end of an alignment of cathedrals representing the Earth as Temple. It was obvious that the royal arch above the two pillars could only take the form of a star constellation. The problem was which one? It was then that I recalled that Roslin village was built at the end of the Great North Road which was called by the Romans 'Lactodorum' – which means the constellation of the Milky Way.

Another piece of this apocalyptic puzzle fell into place when I discovered the reason for the profusion of lilies carved on the barrel vault of the choir above the prentice pillar. For the royal arch above the two pillars at the portal of the original Temple had been decorated with lilies to represent the descending generations of the bloodline of the race of Israel. I was even more excited when I discovered why an equal profusion of stars had been carved beside the lilies. They had been carved to symbolize the stars of the arch of the Milky Way which curved above the as yet unfound configuration for which I was looking.

My last task in Rosslyn was to research the character, personal qualities and career of the founder of Rosslyn. Sir William St Clare (commonly Sinclair), last prince of the Orkneys and Royal Chancellor to the Scottish throne, was a nobleman with singular talents. He was not only the patron of craftmasonry throughout Europe, he was also a grandmaster and an adept of the highest degree. He was born in 1402 at the very beginning of the century which was to see the final decline of the spiritual faculties inherent in the right hemisphere of the brain. More than any other single personality in this period he must have been aware of the real significance of the times in which he lived as a critical turning point in the evolution of human consciousness. And, since recorded history could not inform me on such matters, I attempted as far as I was able to enter his innermost thoughts while the chapel was being built. I pictured this illustrious figure, dressed in the robes of a Scottish nobleman of the fifteenth century, planning the great work in the private rooms of his once imposing castle which is today in ruins. I visualized him supervising the rebuilding of the village which was shortly to house craftsmen of many different skills whom he had called to his service from all parts of Europe. I imagined him busily overseeing his own architectural draft plans of the projected cathedral as they were drawn up piece by piece on Norwegian boards out of which the carpenters made the separate patterns later cut in stone by the masons before the building could begin.

I could not help asking myself a whole series of questions which might appear at first sight to be no more than sheer fantasy or, at best, idle conjecture. Yet the answers to these questions were absolutely vital in my search for the hidden configuration I was hoping to unveil: to what extent had the founder of Rosslyn mastered the ultimate degree of initiation through which the adept transcends the sequence of terrestrial time and can look backwards and forwards through the historical process?

I did not doubt that he anticipated the dawn of rationalism which was already beginning to emerge in his own lifetime. But could he really have envisaged the immense and startling change in human consciousness which was about to take place during the next century when thinking not only sought a new method but also proposed a new aim – to gain power over nature?

To frame these questions in another way: did Lord St Clare actually anticipate the astonishing suddenness with which western man would become united and at home with the forces of the physical world? Did his clairvoyant vision actually foresee the future methods of scientific experiment and investigation, the invention of the machines and the new views of space and time which would lead mankind into a new age? And, if this was the case, did he regard all these things as signs of a greater acuteness of mind or the result of mind itself moving into a new sphere of activity as the left cerebral lobe of the human brain grappled with the mechanical forces of the earth where such triumphs of invention and technique awaited it?

And what did he conceive as the reason for man's gradual descent in the following centuries into a godforsaken world of materialism? Did he believe, as I myself was beginning to think, that mankind could only gain personal freedom as a result of total isolation from the spiritual world? That is to say, did he foresee that man could only become free when his consciousness was entirely cut off from its divine origin? And lastly, did he consider such freedom as a prerequisite for love?

If the real evolutionary purpose for man's confinement to the sense world is to create the possibility for freedom and love, how unlikely it seems that such a brain-fettered imprisonment within three-dimensional awareness is an irreversible process! Did the founder of Rosslyn, who ordered the carving of the wounded brain, anticipate the reanimation of the right hemisphere of the brain and the consequent reawakening of the senses and the faculties of the spirit?

Was it possible that he even expected the hidden configuration, to which he himself was adding the final piece, to be rediscovered with those very spiritual faculties at the end of the second Christian millenium when its apocalyptic significance would be revealed to the world?

The reputation of Lord St Clare as both a historian and a

collector of ancient records is widely known. For instance it is recorded that Sir William, the last Prince of the Orkneys before the title passed to the Scottish Throne, was in possession of the Norse records of the early Viking voyages across the Atlantic to the American Continent. Was it possible, I asked myself, that this last 'Jarl of the Orkneys', envisaging with his unique spiritual faculties a new age of exploration of the globe, sent these records of the epic voyages of Eric the Red and others to Portugal? Did he send them to the Knights of the Order of Christ, the renamed Templar Order, who initiated the age of discovery? Henry the Navigator, the Grandmaster, used its revenues to found the Academy of Nautical Discovery at Sagras which opened up the discovery by sea of both the old world in the east and the new world in the west. It was exciting to consider that the records passing from Scotland to Portugal may not only have anticipated the Age of Discovery but might even have inspired the rediscovery of America.

It seemed likely that the twin pillar for which I was searching was located somewhere in Portugal. The prentice pillar itself had an Orcadian motif. The apprentice himself originally came from the Orkneys and the pillar for which he gave his life represents the Yggdrasill tree of Norse mythology, the world Ash which binds together heaven, earth and hell. The crown of this tree comprises the twelve constellations of the Zodiac, the spiralling branches symbolize the planets and the roots of the trunk dig deeply into the elements of the earth. At the bottom of the pillar the dragons of Neifelheim can be seen gnawing at the roots of the tree to rob it of its fruitfulness. The pillar itself represents a kind of transformation of an ancient pagan conception into the Christian Tree of Life. The next question to be answered concerned the actual locality and the artistic motif of the other pillar, the Tree of Knowledge.

It was time to leave Rosslyn. I packed up and drove south

following the Milky Way through England, France and Spain *en route* to Portugal to find the missing pillar. I searched for it in vain in Sagras around the bleak headland where Henry the Navigator founded his nautical academy. The search proved equally fruitless around the ancient royal residences and tombs, and in the cathedrals and churches of Lisbon and the ancient hill city of Coimbra. Finally, apparently by chance or perhaps led on by the urge to fulfil a personal destiny, I saw the pillar I was looking for as I negotiated the traffic around the square in Cintra, a small town not far from Lisbon.

There it stood some eight feet high with four double spirals of foliage in bas-relief, each different from the other, which wound around the clustered column, bound to it by ropes, at a distance of eighteen inches from one another. Apart from the anti-clockwise direction of the spirals, it was an exact counterpart, the complementary pillar to the prentice pillar in Rosslyn. Unfortunately it was not associated with either a cathedral or a church and its origin was unknown except that it had been carved sometime at the beginning of the fifteenth century. I was jubilant, nevertheless. I had found the two pillars of the apocalyptic configuration in stone.

A strange, new and quite unsuspected relationship to Time and Space began to develop as I travelled back northwards guided by the constellation of the Milky Way above me and the Roman road Lactodorum, now known as the Rue St Jacques, below me. I suddenly realized the search for the Apocalypse in Stone was not unlike the search for the Holy Grail about which I was later to write a book called *The Cup of Destiny*. Now I had the same feeling as the knight Parzifal on Good Friday when he says: 'I have hardly taken a step, yet I feel I have gone far.' I was entering the mystery in which time itself is transformed into space.

Normally in this materialistic age we only consider

Michio - Michael

numbers as an expression of quantity but St John in the Revelation asks us to reckon with the qualitative character of number. For instance, seven is the key number of Time which expresses itself in the whole rhythm of the evolution of consciousness. This is why the whole of the Apocalypse advances entirely in rhythms of seven – the seven stars, the seven golden candlesticks, the seven messages, the seven angels of the seven churches, the seven seals, seven trumpet blasts and the seven vials of wrath.

Sevenfoldness seems to indicate the presence of the Apocalypse. Now I was searching for seven sacred sites which had once been the locations of the seven planetary oracles of the druids. I hoped to find the seven cathedrals of the great configuration located on these seven planetary sites so that their very alignment itself created an apocalyptic constellation against the background of the zodiac.

The druids believed that the seven spirit-senses were not only latent in man himself but also existed as an alignment of Earth Chakras in the body of the planet. The perception of these telluric centres and the knowledge and insight into their working was an integral part of the mystery wisdom of the ancient druids. And this is the reason for the presence of a sequence of seven planetary oracles which were set up in grottoes on seven sacred sites between Iberia and Scotland. The sun oracle, the most important, was located in Carnuntum between the Loire and the Eure, a fact reported by none other than Julius Ceasar in *De Bello Gallico*. Above this sun initiation grotto the cathedral of Notre Dame de Chartres was built. The moon oracle, associated with the mysteries of birth, was situated in northern Spain in the exact place in the Asturias where the body of St James was later buried. Today the carved figure of St James stands above the pillar of birth in the centre of the gate of glory in the magnificent Romanesque Cathedral of Santiago de Compostela, St James of the Field of the Star. At the

69

bottom of this pillar there is a five-pointed star into which millions of pilgrims have placed their fingers.

The Mercury and Venus Oracles of the druids were situated within the Earth Chakras where the cities of Toulouse and Orléans now stand. Above these ancient mystery grottoes today stand their respective cathedrals.*

The Notre Dame de Paris was built beside the Seine on the ancient location of the Mars Oracle, while the Notre Dame in Amiens rests above the grotto where the Celtic priests once initiated their novices into the sublime mysteries of the Jupiter Oracle. Rosslyn Chapel, which was originally planned as a great cathedral, stands upon the sacred site of the Saturn Oracle. Even before the advent of Christianity, druid pilgrims who worshipped the Earth Goddess journeyed from Iberia to Scotland via these planetary oracles associating the alignment of the spirit-senses (organs of clairvoyance) within themselves to the corresponding alignment of the Earth Chakras on the surface of the planet.

It should now be clear why there was no arbitrary choice involved in the discovery as to exactly which seven cathedrals were an integral part of this apocalyptic configuration in stone dedicated to the Goddess Natura, whom St John depicts as the Virgin of the Revelation. The sequence of the sites corresponds to the sequence of the planets in our solar system – Moon, Mercury, Venus, Sun, Mars, Jupiter and Saturn. And each cathedral shows in the sacred geometry of its structure the planetary character of the telluric forces within its locality which it vibrates heavenwards like an ancient dolmen through its towering spires.

It would be quite incorrect to regard this great configura-

---

*The present cathedral in Toulouse in not the original cathedral in the configuration. The original cathedral outside Toulouse was intimately connected with the Cathers and was destroyed. Even the foundations themselves have been all but totally removed.

tion with the two pillars at either end and the seven cathedrals between them under the royal arch of stars as something static like a dead monument in stone. The truth is quite the contrary. Just as subliminal forces stream up and down the alignment of the spirit-senses within the soul-body of man, so similar forces surge northwards and southwards along the great alignment of cathedrals on the surface of the earth. Clairvoyantly perceived, these forces stream and whirl as they fructify the terrain and at the same time create the rainbow aura of the whole configuration. Dowsers, sensitive to earth vibrations, have discovered by their own methods the presence of a leyline passing along this route but unfortunately they have been unable so far to unravel its real significance and purpose.

There is a painting in the Vatican in Rome which throws prophetic light upon these two pillars of the Apocalypse. It is the painting of the Transfiguration of Christ by Raphael, the famous renaissance artist who was at the same time one of the greatest initiates of Christendom. In this painting Raphael depicts Christ transfigured above a mountain. On either side we see Moses and Elijah. Beneath Moses, St James is seen kneeling in the form of an embryo to represent the mysteries of birth. St John is depicted below Elijah in a pose which artists of the period used in order to represent initiation.

Moses looks back into the past towards Genesis, the original creation of earth existence. Elijah, on the other hand, looks prophetically into the future towards the advent of the 'New Jerusalem' of the Revelation. St James is the guide to knowledge which originates from the physical senses and the development of the rational intellect. St John is the guide to the development of spirit vision and spiritual faculties. And when these two disciples perceive the transfigured Christ, they are also seeing a prophetic imagination of the second coming of Christ and the Transfiguration of

71

the Earth which is predicted in the Revelation. It is these two disciples, James and John, who represent the pillars of wisdom and strength, the Tree of Knowledge and the Tree of Life, the two hemispheres of the bicameral mind which will become the two great witnesses of the Apocalypse.

Madonna della Tuvo 18/8/02

CHAPTER SEVEN

THE CHANGING FACE OF INITIATION

Plus ça change, plus c'est la même chose.
The more things change, the more some things remain the same.

To study the process of initiation we need look no further than the history of the mystery school of Chartres. Legend tells how many centuries before the Roman invasion of Gaul the Druids assembling in the region of Chartres for secret ceremonies of initiation received a divine revelation: a virgin was to arise. She would bear a child who was to be the salvation of the world. The Druid initiates erected an altar to this virgin inscribing it with the words later translated into Latin as *Virgini Parturae* (to the virgin who is about to bear) and placed upon an altar a wooden statue of the virgin with child, instituting a cult of worship in her name. When the first Christian missionaries arrived in Chartres they discovered the people were already worshipping the virgin mother and so had little difficulty in converting them to Christianity. The grotto in which the statue was placed was located on a mound above which the cathedral of the Notre Dame de Chartres was later built. The ancient Druidic statue itself rested in the crypt of Chartres Cathedral along with the Robe of Mary and was regarded as an object of veneration by millions of pilgrims until the time of the French Revolution.

Around the year AD 1000 a mystery school was founded in Chartres and developed under the guidance of Bishop Fulbertus to bring about the final flowering of the faculties of the spirit before the critical moment in the fifteenth century when human awareness became fettered to the terrestrial world of the senses. This famous Platonic academy, which was to last almost two hundred years, appeared like a radiant sun illuminating the whole spiritual life of the Middle Ages.

Fulbertus, a great classical scholar, does not appear in character with the Middle Ages of European history. Rather it seems as though a sage of the stature of Socrates had been born out of time from the golden age of ancient Athens. Somehow this great teacher was able to combine the mythology and philosophy of ancient Greece with a heart permeated with Christianity and above all with a reverence for the Virgin Mary which seemed to proceed from the innermost foundation of his soul. His hymns, poems and sermons dedicated to the Virgin gave a new radiance to the festival of the birth of Mary which from this time onward flourished in a new way throughout the whole of Christendom.

It appeared to the medieval mind that fate itself was expressing in an outward historical form the intimate connection of Chartres with the Virgin when, on the eve of Mary's birth, the church and the town itself were burned to the ground. Fulbertus himself undertook the rebuilding of both. The new cathedral, erected with unheard-of splendour, almost immediately exceeded the resources of the bishopric, but such was the reputation and influence of Fulbertus in Rome and throughout the whole of western Europe that his call for help to build anew in honour of the Virgin was richly answered from all quarters.

Following the death of Fulbertus, the central personality in the Christian initiation school in Chartres was Fr Bernardus who gained a reputation as a 'veritable Plato' within the Church during his own lifetime. Besides teaching his students the philosophy, literature, drama and mythology of ancient Greece he also instructed them in initiation techniques which sought to develop the spiritual faculties described in the Revelation of St John. He instructed them regarding the manner in which the Revelation had been *sent in signs* by the angel of God to his servant John. The saying 'sent in signs', Bernardus explained, meant that they must not take the literal meaning of the words as they stand, but seek a deeper meaning of which the words are only signs. It was a Revelation received by St John in the spirit. That which was made manifest to the world in this Revelation was intentionally presented in an exoteric form and they must diligently search within it for a hidden, esoteric, meaning. The pupils of Bernardus underwent a long probation until they were mature enough to understand the true message of the Apocalypse, for the Revelation of St John has the same relation to outward Christianity as the revelations of the initiation mysteries of ancient Greece had to the popular religion and mythology of that time.

Any serious research into this period at the time of Bernardus, when the hidden apocalyptic configuration in stone was built, leads to an awe-inspiring conclusion. And this conclusion is that there are in fact two separate streams of history running parallel to one another. One stream is outwardly visible, the other is hidden to all eyes but those of the initiated. Only the first stream is commonly known as 'history' but hidden behind it at all times is the other stream which continually guides it and shapes it further. This is as true today as it was in the Middle Ages.

Under the guise of studying the seven liberal arts, the pupils of Bernardus developed the seven senses of the spirit. Outwardly they were learning about *gramatica, dialectica, logica, musica, mathematica, geometrica,* and *astronomia,* but these medieval students of the mysteries were also inwardly developing and bringing to fruition the clairvoyant organs

75

which open to a direct vision of the supersensible world. During a long period of probation the students underwent a period of purification in order to overcome the lower and instinctive nature in the soul which blinded them to the existence of the Divine within themselves and within nature. Such purification of the soul discards those elements which prevent it from being harmoniously and regularly organized, thus enabling it to acquire higher organs of perception. Every soul is endowed with the germ of such organs, it is only necessary to bring forth the forces which are present in it. Just as sunlight and water are to a seed the nourishment through which it grows into a flowering plant, so certain feelings and disciplines of thinking and activity are the nourishment to the spiritual organs of the soul. It was these disciplines that were outwardly taught under the guise of the seven liberal arts. After probation and enlightenment, the seven ascending degrees of initiation were gained, leading to a conscious involvement in the spiritual reality that underpins the world of the senses.

The spiritual senses not only unveil to clairvoyant perception the thoughts and mentality, the sentiments and disposition of other souls as well as their talents and capacities, but also give a deeper insight into the laws of all natural phenomena and reveal the very unity in nature which is the mainspring of all creation. It was from this deep understanding of the spiritual realities that underpin the tangible world of nature that the initiates of Chartres divined the importance of the place of the *Goddess Natura* in the Divine plan for man's enlightenment. This is why they carved an exact replica of the statue of the *Virgini Parturae* in the guise of Mary, the Mother of God, on the main portal of the cathedral, from whence it was soon copied not only upon the other cathedrals of the apocalyptic configuration but also on most of the leading cathedrals and churches throughout Christendom. It is perhaps ironic to the

76

uninitiated that one of the major dogmas of present-day Roman Catholicism should have sprung from the spiritual understanding and perception of the hidden initiates of the Middle Ages who were themselves liable to persecution for the heretical nature of their beliefs at that time.

The first visible portent of the critical turning point when humanity reaches the threshold is described in the Revelation as the appearance of the Virgin of the Apocalypse, a woman clothed with the sun, the moon under her feet and her head crowned with stars. Chapter twelve of the Book of Revelation depicts her about to give birth to a child. Below her the figure of a dragon awaits to attempt to devour this child. This vision of the Queen of Heaven, the great Divine Mother who gives birth to her child, did not begin with the Christmas story in Bethlehem.

This vision of the Queen of Heaven was once the universal possession of all peoples. In ancient Egypt man looked up to Isis who bears the Horus Child. The Greeks paid homage to Demeter in Eleusis. And, as we have already described, the Druids too had their madonna, *Virgini Parturae*.

It is the myth of the purified human soul which is revealed here at the very heart of the Revelation. The woman in heaven, who appeared to St John, had already been seen by the atavistic vision of all the ancient peoples. It is the world soul that is described here in the picture of the heavenly mother.

The soul of the universe, the world soul, cannot be visible to our physical eyes or even knowable through intellectual thinking. Although the picture of the woman in heaven had been perceived with the inborn clairvoyance of the ancient civilizations, it was St John who was the first to attain this vision through the faculties of the new initiation. Just as the human soul is a bridge between the individual spirit and the body, so the world soul is the bridge between the spirit world and the terrestrial world, and this is why we divine

77

from the Revelation that mankind will once again under the sign of the heavenly mother be able to open the spiritual, supersensory eye in the same way as the pupils of the mystery school in Chartres perceived the *Goddess Natura.*

The great gift and secret of human existence consists of the fact that every individual person, however tiny a part of the whole cosmos he might be, has within his soul a copy of the world soul. Every human soul is a microcosm corresponding to the great Divine Mother, the soul of the world. The Chartres masters looked into this picture as into a heavenly mirror of their own being, and read from it what God thought when he called human souls into existence. But the child whom the Virgin of the Revelation is about to bear is nothing other than the individual human spirit which is born within the soul of every human being as a 'virgin birth' – the birth of the spiritual male principle from out of the womb of the eternal feminine.

And finally, the initiated sages of Chartres realized that this world soul, the eternal feminine of the entire universe, was now inseparable from Mary, the Mother of God. And this is why they raised her image in the portals of the cathedrals so that she might come close to every human heart. 'Hail Mary, Mother of God.' So that the importance of the Virgin of the Revelation should be recognized by coming generations, at the time when mankind would stand at the very threshold of the spiritual world, the masters of Chartres left us the apocalyptic configuration. This configuration not only gives us a calendar to indicate the time of the main events of the Apocalypse, but also leaves us vital clues as to the role of the Virgin of the Revelation in awakening mankind to supersensible vision. The masters of Chartres envisaged that the main events of the Apocalypse would take place when the terrestrial alignment of the seven cathedrals matched the celestial alignment of the corresponding planets in the heavens above.

The names of the masters of Chartres are known to historians and are a matter of record; this is in complete contrast to the total anonymity of the craftmasons who built the cathedrals in honour of the Virgin and secretly incorporated into their work the fruits of their own hidden initiation cult.

The western Church, anticipating the contraction of human consciousness and inevitable confinement to the terrestrial world, eradicated the conception of the individual spirit from the entelechy of man. As a result of the Council of Nicaea, man was no longer considered to consist of spirit, soul and body but only of body and soul – the spirit being relegated to an intellectual quality in the soul. By eradicating the individual human spirit this Council quite literally closed the gates to the spiritual world for the mass of mankind. Only the hidden Orders of initiates retained the knowledge and capacity for spiritual vision. And the cult which carried the traditions of initiation to the very verge of modern times were the craftmasons.

The demise of the lodges of the craftmasons came at the beginning of the eighteenth century when their own patrons among the aristocracy actively joined in the rituals in the lodges and underwent initiation themselves. Two decades later, around the year AD 1727, the aristocratic initiates changed the password and thus excluded any further participation by the working craftmasons. At this moment what is known today as *Freemasonry* began and changed the nature and purpose of the original craft lodges which had existed in an unbroken line since the building of the Temple of King Solomon in Jerusalem.

The new Freemasonry exposed its aristocratic members to pathways of spiritual knowledge and spiritual faculties which gave them an invaluable insight into the working of earthly power structures. To a privileged class who had lost most of their political power and were reduced to the role of large landowners and courtiers these spiritual insights opened up immense possibilities for political manipulation. The spiritual faculties which had been preserved for moral reasons intended to benefit all mankind were now the exclusive preserve of a privileged clique who used them ruthlessly to gain political power and commercial gain for themselves to exploit the mass of humanity.

There had existed prior to this time an unbroken line of skilled adepts who had guided and trained their novices through every degree in the path of perceptive knowledge. But now this was replaced in most cases by a parrot-like following of the ancient rituals without any clear understanding of their true meaning or effect. Some lodges arose in America, directly connected with the Royal Arch and Rosicrucian degrees of Scottish Masonry, inspired by the model of Rosslyn. Among them were supremely gifted men of great spiritual insight and moral force. These perceptive and powerful men left a lasting imprint on what has become modern society. The gift of the Constitution of the United States of America – the legal foundation for all the basic values of freedom, democracy and the rights of man is the lasting spiritual legacy that we have received from this branch of Freemasonry. But in some of the highest and most exclusive lodges control was taken over by black adepts who by this means entered the international arena of politics and began to corrode these high moral and spiritual aims.

The cosmic Christianity of the Revelation of St John has one thing in common for the white and the black adepts of Freemasonry. Through their rituals they enter spiritual realms with divine or demonic motivation under the same 'Open Heaven' of the Apocalypse, from which the veil has been rent, and in which closed intellectual speculation has neither power nor validity. For the moral aspirant, who has devoutly and patiently prepared his soul by ritual disciplines and meditation, the veil is legitimately rent from 'top to bottom' as an act of grace by the Christian time spirit. Black adepts must tear away the veil from below upwards with their own magic rituals and satanic arts. Yet both the good and the evil adepts must pass through the same curtain of the sense world into the same higher dimensions of time and consciousness and share a vision and participation in the same supersensible world. And yet both also wear city suits, collars and ties and, without penetrating occult insight, it is impossible on the contemporary scene to differentiate between the two. Yet when the history of our century is later seen in its true perspective in the evolution of human consciousness it will be fully realized that this is the true arena of conflict between the powers of good and evil which will decide the ultimate fate of humanity.

Most Freemasons, who considered themselves to be good men and true, were quite unaware of the presence of the evil motives at work behind the most powerful lodges in Europe and America. To give an apparent air of respectability to their schemes, the black adepts encouraged the charitable actions of the well-intentioned but deluded majority of their fellow members and welcomed membership from the most high; Kings and senior officials becoming Grand Masters of the most exclusive lodges and the unwitting tools of evil powers who used their involvement as an instrument of national and international exploitation.

Freemasonry became an indispensable key to high office. For instance, every Prime Minister in England, from Walpole in the eighteenth century to Ramsey MacDonald in the twentieth century, was a Grand Master of the Freemason order. This pattern of power was repeated throughout Europe. The same situation also existed in America where every President until John F. Kennedy was a Freemason of a high degree. This domination of power was not just restricted to the Heads of State but also permeated throughout the entire power structures of the judiciary, the police, the armed services and civil administration of the western world.

The divine inspiration in the realm of the crafts had come to an end. Excluded from their own lodges, the working craftmasons formed guilds which later developed into the craft trade unions and what later became the labour movement. This exclusion from the mysteries not only brought a fundamental change in their attitudes to work but also in the new organization into which they grouped themselves. The fruits of their anonymous labours which had been dedicated *Ad Majorem Dei Gloriam* now became simply the end results of craft skills which had to compete in the marketplace with other products of the commercial world. Skilled human labour had now become a commodity which could be sold like any other product.

Now at the threshold of the spiritual world this tragic division in humanity confronts the twofold face of evil in separate ways. The ruling classes are inspired by the power seeking of Lucifer; and the workers whom they exploit are blinded to the spirit and hurled into the materialistic embrace of Ahriman. And so as a result of this division between the rulers and the ruled, the foundations for the present development of the East–West confrontation between the opposing ideologies of Capitalism and Communism were laid.

CHAPTER EIGHT

THE KEY TO THE UNVEILING OF PERSONAL DESTINY

There are more things in heaven and earth, Horatio,
Than are dreamt of in your philosophy.

Hamlet: William Shakespeare

All the world's a stage,
And all the men and women merely players:
They have their exits and their entrances;
And one man in his time plays many parts,
His acts being seven ages. At first the infant,
Mewling and puking in his nurse's arms,
And then the whining school-boy, with his satchel,
And shining morning face, creeping like snail
Unwillingly to school.

As You Like It: William Shakespeare

It is a bizarre situation that man in the twentieth century should be on the one hand hurled by the apocalyptic events of the time against the threshold of the spiritual world and at the same moment be in a condition of almost total blindness to spiritual reality. Traditional paths to initiation no longer have any relevance to the present condition of human consciousness in which man has been completely severed from all indications of spiritual reality in order to develop that freedom which is a pre-requisite for love. The only way ahead now is a path to self knowledge which will transcend the barriers of birth and death and reveal the meaning of personal destiny.

What we admire in the character of a genius is his ability to pierce through the semblance of the moment, reawaken the past and point out clear paths to the future. The significance of the claimants to the Spear of Destiny has been this very capacity for insight into the requirements of their time; a perception of the nascent principle, the necessary, directly sequential step in progress for the age they lived in. It is for this reason too that mankind stands in awe of St John who gave us his Revelation from an unbroken circle of time, presenting us with endless vistas of the past and the future as though time itself had become visible space. It seems as though he speaks out of a higher dimension of time in which past, present and future are a single continuous whole. And it is along this path towards the experience of a higher time-dimension that humanity must now tread. The Spear of Longinus is the symbol of this new way of initiation which transcends birth and death and reveals the true meaning of personal destiny, the meaning of the sequential events and relationships in the life of each individual.

The freedom that is a pre-requisite for love carries within it an awesome responsibility to others, especially at the moment an individual involves himself in this new path of initiation, because there is no longer the code of behaviour or the vows that were imposed by the ancient masters of the mysteries. Many young people today misguidedly go off in search of masters in order to obtain enlightenment.

It is a tragedy of modern times that there are so many gurus to lead them away from true development, yet most people seem to end up with what they deserve and are forced as a result to reassess their motives. On the other hand, everyone may be certain that initiation will find them under all circumstances if they pursue a path to self knowledge in which their very motives give proof of an earnest and worthy endeavour to unveil the real meaning of their lives. In considering the conditions which the novice should impose upon himself it is not their complete fulfilment which is most important, but only the corresponding effort. No one is expected to wholly fulfil them, yet all students can at least start on the path towards their accomplishment.

The first condition is that the student should take heed towards the advancement of bodily and spiritual health. Of course, health does not depend in the first place on the individual; but the effort to improve in this respect lies within the scope of all. Sound knowledge can only proceed from sound human beings – *'Mens sana in corpore sano'*. Many people ascribe to their circumstances everything which apparently stops them making progress. They object that such development is not possible under the conditions they live in. Perhaps many may find it desirable for other reasons to change their conditions of life, but no one need do so for the purpose of unveiling the meaning of their own destiny. Every kind of work can serve the whole of humanity; and it is a surer sign of greatness of soul to perceive clearly how necessary for this whole is a petty, perhaps even a boring form of employment than to think: 'This work is not good enough for me. I'm destined for something better.' Of special importance is the striving for complete health of mind. An unhealthy life of thought and feeling will not fail to obstruct the path to higher knowledge. Clear, calm thinking with stability of feeling and emotion form here the basis of all work. All inclination towards exaggeration and fanaticism should be eradicated. The student should meet the demands of life with steady assurance, quietly letting all things make their impression on him and reveal their message. All one-sided and extravagant tendencies in sentiment and criticism should be avoided. Failing this, the novice would merely find his way into worlds of his own imagination where instead of spiritual realities asserting themselves pet opinions take their place. In short it is better on this path to be matter-of-fact to the point of dullness than to be excitable and fantastic.

The second condition is that the student of destiny should feel himself co-ordinated as a link in the whole of life. Much is included in the fulfilment of this condition. Instead of directing his feelings against others, the student should reflect at all times on his own attitude, and in such a way his whole way of thinking will be changed. This holds good in all things great or small. Such an attitude of mind, for instance, alters the way we might regard a criminal. If we suspend our judgement and say to ourselves: 'We are, after all, like him, only human beings. Through favourable circumstances we have received a family background and an education which has perhaps saved us from a similar fate.' We may then come to the conclusion that this human brother of ours would have become a different person had his teachers worked with the same love and affection as they did with us. We can reflect that something was given to us that was withheld from him, and that we enjoy our good fortune precisely because it was denied to him. Out of this outlook, the student comes to think of himself as a link in the whole of humanity and a sharer in the responsibility for everything that occurs. Of course, this does not imply that such thoughts should be immediately translated into action or external acts of agitation. Rather the new attitude should be cherished in stillness within the soul. Gradually it will set its mark on the outward demeanour of the student who now realizes that he must begin by reforming himself.

The third condition guides the student to the realization that his thoughts and feelings are as important for the world as his actions. He must realize that it is equally injurious to hate a fellow being as to strike him. And from this realization it follows that by perfecting ourselves we accomplish something not only for ourselves but also for the whole world. The world derives equal benefit from our untainted feelings as from our good demeanour, and as long as we cannot believe in the universal importance of our own inner life we are unfit to develop the faculties which will unveil the secrets of the personal destiny of other souls. We are only filled with the right significance of our own soul life when we work at it as though it were at least as important as all external things.

The fourth condition requires the conviction that the real being of man does not lie in his exterior but in his interior. Anybody regarding himself wholly as a product of the outer world, that is as a result of the physical world only, cannot succeed on this path. The feeling that we are also beings of soul and spirit forms its very basis.

The acquisition of this feeling renders the student of destiny fit to distinguish between inner duty and outer success. He will learn very quickly that one cannot be measured directly by the other. He must find the proper mean between what is indicated by external conditions and what he recognizes as right for himself. He should not force upon his environment anything for which he can have no understanding, but he must also be quite free from the desire to do only that which will please those around him. The voice of his own soul struggling honestly for self knowledge must be his only guide. Yet he must learn as much as possible from his environment in order to discover what those around him need, and what is good for them. In this way he will develop within himself a spiritual balance; an open heart for the needs of the outer world on one hand, and an inner fortitude and an unfaltering endurance on the other.

The fifth condition concerns steadfastness in carrying out a resolution. Nothing should induce the student on his way to initiation to deviate from a resolution he may have taken, save only the perception that he was in error. Every resolution is a force, and if this force does not produce an immediate effect at the point to which it applied it works nevertheless in its own way. Success is only decisive when an action arises from desire. But all actions arising from desire alone are worthless in relation to the spiritual worlds to which the student is seeking entry. There, love for an action is the sole decisive factor. In this love every impulse that impels the student to action should fulfil itself. Undismayed by failure, he will never grow weary of endeavouring repeatedly to translate some resolution into action. And in this way he reaches the stage of not waiting to see the outward effect of his actions but of contenting himself with performing them. He will learn to sacrifice his actions, even his very life itself, to the world however the world may receive his sacrifice. Readiness for sacrifice for others is essential for all those who wish to unveil the laws that govern human destiny.

The sixth condition is the development of a feeling for everything with which man is favoured. Our existence is a gift from the entire universe. How much is needed to enable each one of us to receive and maintain his existence! Thoughts such as these must come quite naturally to those who tread the new path towards enlightenment. Anyone who does not feel inclined towards such gratitude will be incapable of developing within himself that all-embracing love which is necessary for the attainment of the spiritual knowledge which arises as a result of higher consciousness. Nothing can reveal itself to us that we do not love. And every revelation must fill us with thankfulness, for we ourselves are richer for it.

The seventh condition demands that we regard life unceasingly in the manner demanded by all these conditions. In this manner the student makes it possible to give his life the stamp of uniformity. All his modes of expression will, in this way, be brought into harmony, and no longer conflict or contradict each other. And thus he will prepare himself for the inner tranquillity to contemplate his own life with complete objectivity.

The key to unveiling a higher time-dimension which can review both life before birth and life after death, thus breaching the natural barriers which conceal the spiritual world, is a systematized and progressive technique of time reversal. Time reversal in this context appears at first to be such a simple activity that one is inclined to discount it as a catalyst to higher consciousness. However simple it may first appear, it is, on the contrary, remarkably difficult to carry out effectively. Once mastered, it not only proves to be the most important single factor in raising the quality and intensity of consciousness and in unveiling higher time dimensions, it also prepares the soul for the implosion of supersensible awareness and orientates it to the anatomy of inner space.

What we are also achieving here in the life of the soul is a new and magical form of meditation – a technique of sense-free thinking which is combined with memories of our own terrestrial life in the sense world. We have illustrated at some length how the left brain can only reflect into consciousness that which can be perceived by the senses. It is for this reason that the left brain activity comes to a stand-still as a result of sense-free imaginative thinking, while the right brain is both nurtured and developed by this very activity. It is the technique of time reversal which combines the activities of both sides of the brain and at the same time allows us to look down into a three-dimensional world from outside it.

All that is immediately required in this technique is to review each night the personal activities and events of the day in the reverse order to which they originally took place. There are certain obvious technical difficulties in achieving this because it is necessary to see yourself from outside as though you were a stranger. Except when looking into a mirror, it is never possible to see one's own face, gestures, stance and mannerisms. Something of the artistic imagination of the painter is needed here in order to insert yourself from outside into your own memory images. Somehow in reviewing any moment or event in the day you must select the best external viewpoint from which imaginatively to paint one's own physical form, features and gestures from outside. Nevertheless with a little regular practice each night before you go to bed it can very quickly be accomplished.

There is another obstacle of a different nature which is to overcome the reluctance of the soul to contemplate and assess its own feelings, personal experiences, indeed its whole inner life, as though belonging to another. The view we generally take of the experiences and actions of other people differs from the view we take of our own. It happens this way because we are a part of our own experience and actions, while we merely observe those of another. You may have already realized that the object of this painful exercise is to see ourselves as others see us – in such a manner to depersonalize and objectify our otherwise very personal and subjective soul life.

The most persistent obstacle along this path is in the realm of emotion and feeling, because such self contemplation demands that all feelings of guilt and shame as well as other personal recriminations are set aside. To maintain any dogmatic beliefs, prescribed moral attitudes and preconceived ideas can only have an adverse effect. It is vital that a quite new range of feelings and moral insights must be permitted to arise spontaneously as a result of such a totally objective review of each passing day.

When such regular self contemplation is carried out with due care and singleness of mind it has the most salutary effect on personal life and very quickly yields fruitful results. One thing which is immediately noticed is a new edge to self awareness, bringing an awakening of social responsibility, especially in regard to the spoken word, a defined sense of purpose and an increase in resolution.

A new tranquillity of mind and body arises during the period set aside for such contemplation, and the novice soon becomes aware of heightening powers of concentration. The practitioner will also soon discover that the natural and necessary corollary to this exercise is to set aside periods each morning to plan as far as possible the activities and events of the new day. When this early morning exercise is also established as a habit, the first glimpse of the working of human destiny is revealed by the intrusion of unpredicted events for which one can never plan and very rarely anticipate.

The serious student now begins to review the whole of his life with the same exacting and objective self contemplation working back from the present, month by month, towards childhood. He contemplates his inner life and outer behaviour through the years with serene detachment. And he brings to this activity all the energy, inner truthfulness and uncompromising sincerity he can muster.

Every thought, every word, every action, every resolve, and all joys and sorrows, cares, experiences, interests and ambitions finally begin to appear in a new light. Now it seems that he is indeed contemplating the life of a stranger. The very measure of personal egoism and the real nature of motivation are now revealed to him. The participant may well be astonished to discover just how ludicrous a false pride and arrogance have up to now remained hidden from him. No longer entangled in illusions about his past, he is able, without fear, guilt or shame, to separate the essential from the non-essential, the morally real from the unreal. Such self knowledge, although initially painful, leads to an immense release of vital energy.

Another important discovery to be made through such rigorous self contemplation is the true relationship between feeling and cognition. One is inclined somewhat carelessly to regard cognition as an isolated faculty existing of itself without any immediate connection with other faculties within the human psyche. It is all too easy to overlook the fact that it is the soul itself which exercises the faculty of cognition. And that, in this respect, human feelings are to the soul what food is to the body. It is a simple matter to recognize that the body becomes frail and weak when it is starved of nourishment. But just how many of us are inclined to disregard the fact that feelings of wonder, goodwill, respect, admiration and devotion are the nourishment which bring health and vigour to the soul – and especially to the faculty of cognition itself.

The converse is also true. Disrespect, antipathy, adverse criticism, underestimation, contempt and hatred exercise a paralysing and withering effect on the very manner in which we perceive the world around us. This is why it is essential to focus on the refinement of feeling and cultivate reverence and devotion until the recesses of the soul are irradiated with a consecrated fire of love which in its turn will infuse all sense experience with a fresh and radiant quality. Through the very magic of this technique the soul becomes a witness to a nature transfigured with Eden brightness.

All visual impressions are immeasurably intensified and the whole experience of colour is heightened. The golden sunlight, the blue of the sky and the green of the grass are perceived with newly awakened eyes. An eternal quality is sensed even in the very transiency of wild flowers, ripening corn and the song of the birds. In such a way the soul gradually learns to discriminate between the eternal and the ephemeral with a perception cleansed of egoism and rejoicing in the artistry of creation.

The novice's review of his life, which has now become transformed into a process of moral recollection (in the true Platonic sense of the word), now enters a new phase when he begins to recall the scenes of his childhood in vivid pictures. At last he reaches a barrier beyond which he cannot remember, that moment in which the first experience of the 'I' flashed up within him – the very point at which physical memory begins. He does not give up at this point but adamantly continues the struggle, striving yet harder to reach back into yet more tender years of childhood. But for this vital step something else is needed in addition to self contemplation.

Even when a man has learned to confront himself as a complete stranger, it is only himself that he contemplates; he looks on those experiences and actions with which he is connected through his station and particular circumstances in life. He must now disengage himself from it and rise to a purely human level which no longer has anything to do with his own particular situation. He must pass on to the contemplation of those things which would concern him as a human being even if he lived under quite different circumstances. And in this way something begins to live within him which ranges above the purely personal. He begins to experience that his soul is the bridge between two worlds, the physical and the spiritual. And thus he begins to feel and to realize, as a direct inner experience, that he belongs to higher levels of reality, to spiritual worlds concerning which the physical senses and deductive intellectual thinking can tell him nothing.

Gradually the novice reaches the point when he becomes aware that a higher self, an individual human spirit, is now coming to birth within him of which his former egoistic self was but a shadow. He is experiencing the birth of an eternal reality, that spirit-self which will lead him beyond the boundaries of life and death. As a result he now shifts the central point of his being to the inner part of his nature. It is meditation which raises the soul to union with the spirit and brings the eternal fully to birth within him. The existence of this eternal being which transcends birth and death can only be doubted by those who have not themselves experienced it.

The revelation which the student is seeking, and which is brought closer through the disciplines of meditation, may happen at the moment of awakening or even in the middle of his daily activities. He suddenly finds himself looking down upon a small child. But now he has no need to recall his own memory images of childhood in pursuance of his long-practised technique. For he himself is now united with the spirit, his own individual human spirit, looking down on his own tiny body as he had indeed once looked down upon it throughout his early childhood.

It is precisely the opposite experience to the manner in which as an adult he sees the world through the windows of the physical senses, using the brain to reflect upon what he sees. That is to say, he is no longer trapped within length, breadth and thickness but is outside this three-dimensional continuum, living holistically in the immediate surroundings of his childhood with a sublime participatory consciousness.

Such is the working of this sublime transcendent consciousness that he can only describe it by saying that he feels himself to be wholly united with everything he sees. For instance he even experiences his mother, sisters and brothers and childhood friends from inside, as though he is totally united and identified with them. Nature too reveals all her innermost secrets to him in a godlike manner from every point on the periphery, at once effortlessly grasping the totality of her living relationships and experiencing everything with immediacy.

However, the most essential aspect of this experience for the novice must concern the infant below him, in whom his own awareness of the earthly 'I' will shortly flash forth to a perception of the sense world at the expense of the dwindling consciousness of the spirit. Not for nothing has this experience been likened to the fall from paradise, the dreadful expulsion from the Garden of Eden.

In complete fascination – for he has now carried back his purified earthly 'I' into the heights of the spirit – he knows that he does not yet see with the eyes of the child below him whom he must shortly and inevitably become. Nor does he hear with the ears of the child, move with his limbs or clutch out with his tiny hands. He still dwells serenely above the body into which he will shortly incarnate to grapple in spiritual blindness with the terrestrial world. It needs the genius of a poet to find words with which to describe the reality behind such an experience. The little-known words of Thomas Traherne (1637–74), which shows him to have had a memory capable of reaching back to the pre-natal origins of the soul, describe this experience in beautiful imagery. But we will begin by quoting 'The Ode on Intimations of Immortality from Recollections of Early Childhood' by William Wordsworth. It is known to very many people in the western world, yet this may well be the first time that most of them perceive it as a description of reality and not merely a piece of poetic fantasy:

Our birth is but a sleep and a forgetting:
The Soul that rises with us, our life's Star

Hath had elsewhere its setting,
And cometh from afar:
Not in entire forgetfulness,
And not in utter nakedness,
But trailing clouds of glory do we come
From God who is our home:
Heaven lies about us in our infancy!
Shades of the prison-house begin to close
Upon the growing Boy,
But he beholds the light, and whence it flows,
He sees it in his joy;
The Youth, who daily farther from the East
Must travel, still is Nature's Priest,
And by the vision splendid
Is on his way attended; ...
... Hence, in a season of calm weather,
Though inland far we be,
Our Souls have sight of that immortal sea
Which brought us hither,
Can in a moment travel thither
And see the Children sport upon the shore,
And hear the mighty waters rolling evermore.

It is tragic that Wordsworth in his later years did not retain in full consciousness the earliest experiences of childhood. But Thomas Traherne shows us that he retained with him throughout his entire life the very nature of his soul in his earliest years:

Certainly Adam in Paradise had not more sweet and curious apprehensions of the world, than when I was a child.

All appeared new, and strange at first, inexpressibly rare and delightful and beautiful. I was a little stranger, which at my entrance into the world was saluted and surrounded with innumerable joys. My knowledge was Divine. I knew by intuition those things which since my Apostasy, I collected again by the highest reason.... I was entertained like an Angel with the works of God in their splendour and glory, I saw all in the peace of Eden; Heaven and Earth did sing my Creator's praises, and could not make more melody to Adam, than to me. All time was Eternity, and a perpetual Sabbath. Is it not strange, that an infant should be heir to the whole World, and see those mysteries which the books of the learned never unfold?

'A Child's Vision of the World', *Centuries of Meditations*

This same experience comes to a more complete expression in poetic form in Traherne's poem 'Wonder':

How like an Angel came I down!
How bright are all things here!
When first among his works I did appear.
Oh, how their glory did me crown!
The world resembled his eternity,
In which my soul did walk;
And every thing that I did see
Did with me talk.

The following passage from 'The Preparative' not only gives a detailed picture of the condition of the human soul before descending into the terrestrial senses of the body, but even beyond this it describes the soul's experience of embryonic life:

My Body being dead, my Lims unknown;
Before I skild to prize
Those living Stars, mine Eys;
Before my Tongue or Cheeks were to me shewn,
Before I knew my Hands were mine,
Or that my Sinews did my Members joyn,
When neither Nostril, Foot, nor Ear,
As yet was seen, or felt, or did appear;
I was within
A House I knew not, newly clothd with Skin.

Then was my Soul my only All to me,
A living endless Ey
Just bounded with the Skie,
Whose Power, whose Act, whose Essence was to see.

Our novice has not yet got as far as this towards his goal – full union of the soul with the spirit. He must still persevere on what is now for him beyond all doubt the truly effective path towards unveiling the meaning of personal destiny. He must not rest in the joys and pleasures of his newly gained insights but use them for gaining strength to pass back gradually through his earliest childhood towards the moment of birth. And the moment of illumination will astonish him more profoundly than anything he has yet experienced.

One morning upon waking, or at some less convenient hour of the day, he will find himself looking down on his own adult body in what seems to him to be an experience of death. And now, caught up in an immeasurably heightened awareness, he will see whirls of spiral light burst forth from it to form a mosaic of living pictures comprising a mighty tableau he must clothe it in his own *Extra-Percipient-Fantasy*, somewhat like an artist working his conceptions

Perhaps for the first few moments he or she will be overcome by shock, but wonder and interest will quickly gain control as the multi-coloured vision grows ever larger and larger, yet retaining the same internal proportions as though it were painted on the inside of an ever-expanding dome.

He will not behold this panorama of his life with anything even remotely similar to earthly senses but with a newly awakened faculty which he cannot yet clearly understand. It is in fact the faculty of *Imaginative Cognition* which we have already described in our previous pages regarding the Seals of the Apocalypse. This faculty will be immedi-

98

ately recognized as a form of cognition in which a controlled and directed imagination itself becomes an actual means of perception. To behold the unfolding tableau he must clothe it in his own *Extra-Percipient-Fantasy*, somewhat like an artist working his conceptions in paint in order to perceive them on the canvas.

The memory tableau is not a three-dimensional entity of length, breadth and thickness. Rather it appears that a fourth dimension has turned the novice's memory inside out to give it a magical physiognomy in which inward response to outer events is made visible along with the events themselves.

The panorama is also an experience of a new dimension because the events in the unfolding mosaic are not simply a spatial projection of memory images appearing in the succession in which they originally took place. The images are separated into specific clusters of cause and effect which are dictated by the hidden laws of destiny. To perceive any specific event is at the same time to experience it with all the intensity with which it originally took place. And, although one is able to re-experience each event separately, the whole tableau is in itself a time unity, just as musical notes in a certain time relationship are experienced as a melody.

The novice has previously regarded time as a medium within which he experienced events in succession. Now he sees how time is in reality a part of his own being, welding the events of his life into an unbroken whole. He now conceives himself to be a 'Time Being' and he recognizes the expanding tableau as a 'Time Organism'.

At this moment a new realization comes to him, the implications of which lead to what the intellect could only regard as contradictory and bizarre conclusions. He sees beyond contradiction that 'Time' and 'Life' are as inseparable as two sides of a coin. The expanding time organism had formerly acted as his own life organism – a complex of

99

forces which had formed and developed his physical body and informed and sustained it throughout his terrestrial existence – indeed the very life forces which are even now leaving it, to fan out like a script of spatial imagery into the pictorial story of his life.

As he looks down upon his own body, the novice is under the impression that he is dead. The whole drama of his manhood, youth, childhood and infancy is spreading out before him like 'such stuff as dreams are made of' and he is reviewing each of his motives, thoughts, feelings, words and deeds with the impartiality, detachment and heightened moral insight of the spirit. While he reviews the tableau, he understands with immediacy how he had been unwittingly living out a prescribed pattern of personal destiny throughout his life on earth; hidden laws working from earlier incarnations dictating the nature and sequence of events in his life as well as selecting the people with whom he should share it.

He can now see with the faculty of inspiration a whole new dimension of meaning within his life tableau, which no longer appears only as a pattern of events but above all as a web of human relationships in which he had aided or obstructed the spiritual growth of others towards self knowledge. It becomes evident to him that moral laws rule the destiny of mankind. And, from a heightened perception of the working of these laws as seen from the standpoint of the spirit, he is now forced to assess the moral worth of his own life and sit in judgement on himself.

There is one aspect of this chastening experience which puzzles him greatly and for which he can at first find no satisfactory explanation. The panorama of his life appears to include events beyond the present moment which lead on into the future. Only slowly does he grasp that he is not after all dead but undergoing a vital form of spiritual illumination. As this conviction gains strength the tableau recedes beyond the moment of birth and through the womb of his physical creation into the blessed pristine innocence of pre-natal existence. He has transcended the mortal time barriers of birth and death to discover himself as a spirit among spirits. And above all else he knows himself to be a Spirit of the Light:

> I was an Inward Sphere of Light,
> Or an Interminable Orb of Sight
> An Endless and a Living Day,
> A vital Sun that round about did ray
> All Life, All Sense,
> A Naked, Simple, Pure Intelligence.

Ibid

At this moment of spiritual illumination it becomes immediately apparent that each individual person is living out a prescribed pattern of fate and that the only freedom within this life tableau rests in the inward reaction at each moment to events and relationships as they arise. The manner in which the human soul reacts to its fate in one life creates the karmic pattern of the next. This is the primal law at work in reincarnation.

One definite achievement along this path to self knowledge which unveils the meaning of destiny is that it completely transforms the thinking, feeling and volition of the practitioner. Thinking becomes so objective that it serves the human Spirit; feeling becomes so purified and de-personalized that it transforms the soul into a vessel of Love; the human will, no longer directed towards personal satisfaction, becomes the servant of a power greater than ourselves, Almighty God himself. Man is no longer a slave of the entelechy of thinking, feeling and volition. He has put aside the threads which bound him and becomes a free individual spirit whose single conscious motive is the service of the spiritual world.

101

The greatest example of such a loving and willing submission to the will of God was the acceptance by Christ of the sacrificial ritual at Golgotha. Such was his total and absolute submission to the will of the Father that legend recalls how the Roman soldiers who performed the execution were unclear as to whether Christ's hands opened to the nails or whether the nails pierced the hands. To such an extent did He accept His fate at the hands of mankind as the supremely innocent vessel of redemption.

The magic of the Holy Lance for the individual rests in the fact that the nail secured within the blade of the Spear holds the answer to the riddle of the working of both fate and free will. For this reason anybody who interests himself in the historical significance of the Spear finds that its influence evokes questions about human destiny. This is why we have named it 'The Spear of Destiny'.

A nail from the crucifixion of Christ was inserted into a central aperture in the blade of the Spear of Destiny in the thirteenth century. The nail was secured with separate metal threads composed of Gold, Silver and Copper which symbolized not only the human entelechy but also the Holy Trinity of Father, Son and Holy Spirit. This was inspired as a result of the Grail knowledge which conceived that fate befell to man out of the necessity of the Father God, whilst the possibility of human freedom stemmed from the sacrificial love of the Son. A man was led into debt and illusion when he failed to understand how fate and freedom were intermingled in human destiny. He achieved blessedness only when he discovered how divinely regulated fate (or Karma) and human freedom together ruled his personal destiny.

The Spear of Destiny is the symbol of the Apocalypse because the blade represents fate, the working of the law of moral consequence which transforms the happenings of earlier centuries into new patterns of world events. The nail enclosed in the blade symbolizes how the destiny of each individual is inextricably bound into the fabric of the historical process. In this manner the Spear of Destiny reveals how the drama and symbolism of history is a result of the interweaving of personal reincarnation patterns.

CHAPTER NINE

THE DRAMA AND SYMBOLISM OF HISTORY AS THE RESULT OF THE INTERWEAVING OF REINCARNATION PATTERNS

Jesus began to speak to the crowd about John ... 'And if you are willing to accept it, he is the Elijah who was to come. He who has ears, let him hear.'

St Matthew (New International Version) 11: verses 7, 14 and 15

Certain is death to the born, and rebirth to the dead.

Bhagavad Gita

The process of reincarnation is illustrated by the previous lives of various historical figures. The sequence of their lives not only unveils their spiritual biography, but also indicates how their spiritual growth in one life is continued in their successive appearances on earth. Our examples are not contemporary because it is not permissible to disclose the previous incarnations of living people.

We have chosen heroic figures who have played leading roles in history and fulfilled definite missions throughout the passing centuries. Our own reincarnations as ordinary people also play a part in lesser roles in the interweaving of the tapestry of the ongoing historical process. Each person, great or small, will discover that their own individual reincarnation pattern answers the spiritual needs of their own unfolding destiny so that for them also history becomes a truly personal affair.

When Winston Churchill strode towards Buckingham Palace in 1940 to accept the post of Prime Minister he later described how he felt he was walking with destiny and that the whole of his life had been but a preparation for this moment. The truth was, had he known it, that the sequence of all his previous lives on earth had been a preparation for the first apocalyptic battle between good and evil in which he was to play such a decisive part.

Winston Churchill's reincarnations are revealed in the same cosmic chronicle from which St John wrote the Revelation. Access to the Akashic Record has been open to genuine initiates of all cultures since the beginning of recorded history. It was with the requisite faculties of initiation that St John unfurled vast vistas of the past and the future in which the drama and symbolism of history is the result of the interweaving of reincarnation patterns.

The spiritual biography of the soul we knew as Winston Spencer Churchill reveals that he was the very first champion of democracy when it originally appeared in ancient Greece two thousand four hundred years ago. At that time he was incarnate as Pericles, the greatest single figure of the golden age who destroyed the power of the few élite families by appealing to the popular vote. It was Pericles who rebuilt the city after the first Persian invasion, and conceived and masterminded the construction of the Acropolis through which he believed Athens would become an immortal city. In his previous life Pericles had been Priam, the king of Troy, whose defeat by the ancient Greeks had been recorded by Homer in the epic form of the *Iliad*. Now Pericles faced invasion from the east and founded the navy that would defeat the Persian invasion. To protect the Athenian trade routes he sent an expedition to fortify the area now known as Gallipoli, the very place where Winston Churchill was to plan one of the most bloody and unsuccessful campaigns of the First World War. Pericles gained power because he was the first great political orator who used his skills to manipulate the popular vote, a vote which finally turned against him in his declining years.

All the leading figures in ancient Greece reappear as important personalities in the rise and fall of the Roman Empire, Pericles returning as the greatest champion of Roman democracy, Gnaeus Pompeius Magnus – Pompey the Great. Pompey used his political and military skills to support Sulla in the civil war through which power was effectively transferred from the leading patrician families to the Senate. One of the greatest statesmen, generals and reformers of the late Roman Republic he was renowned as an orator and a lawmaker who founded the Roman navy and cleared the Mediterranean of pirates. One of his most tragic mistakes was his support of Herod the Great to become King of Israel. Even in his physical appearance he bears a strong likeness to Winston Churchill, a resemblance that does not end there, for like Churchill he was a great patriot and a man of scholarly achievement and an associate of both Greek and Roman *literati*. It was the destiny of this soul in the days of the final decline of the Roman Empire to reincarnate as Boethius who gave to the world *The Consolations of Philosophy* as a résumé of the ethical thinking of the classical world.

When the separate nations of Europe began to emerge, as a result of the settlement of migrating peoples in the eighth and ninth centuries, the heroic figures of Greece and Rome reappeared on earth to bring the epic leadership which would mould the folksouls of the different peoples. For instance, Caesar Augustus reappears as Charlemagne, the leader of the Franks and the first Holy Roman Emperor. While it was Julius Caesar, who once conquered Gaul, that now defends the same territory against the Arab invasion as Karl the Hammer, the warrior who vanquished Abdul Rahman and his hordes between Tours and Poitiers. The individual who had originally been alive on earth as Pericles and Pompey descends again as Alfred the Great, the founder of the English nation.

Alfred the Great, the youngest of four children, anticipated the life of a scholar but destiny was to make him not only king but the champion of the Saxon peoples in their fight against the invading Danes. When all was apparently lost and most of the Saxons had submitted to the invaders it was Alfred who secretly mustered his own army. He not only conquered the Danes but also Christianized and absorbed them into the emerging English nation. He was the first English king to organize what later developed into the English navy. This descendant of Charlemagne not only rose to fame as a warrior king but is also remembered as a scholar who translated the works of Boethius and many other Latin works, including the scriptures, into the English language. He also instituted the beginning of the Anglo-Saxon Chronicle which, together with the works of Bede, forms the foundation of English history. History remembers him not only as a leader who won victory in hopeless circumstances but also as a great lawmaker. The central study of Alfred's life, the relation of predestination to free will, would later give Winston Spencer Churchill his own pronounced sense of personal destiny.

It was just such another quirk of destiny that Alfred the Great would reincarnate as John Churchill, later the Duke of Marlborough, son of the first Sir Winston Churchill MP. An even greater quirk of destiny was that Britain's greatest wartime leader, Sir Winston Spencer Churchill, was born in the bed of the first Duke of Marlborough who was one of his own previous incarnations!

The drama and symbolism of history is most visible as a result of reincarnation patterns when a great individual relives in his present life the rhythmical patterns of his previous incarnations. The career of Sir Winston Spencer

107

Churchill gives us an insight into this process in which central and recurrent themes can clearly be seen arising from the lives of Pericles, Pompey, Boethius, Alfred the Great and the Duke of Marlborough. Running through all their lives are the great central themes – the championship of democracy, a mastery of naval strategy, strategic and tactical ability applied to great patriotic idealism, periods of prolonged unpopularity in the political wilderness and, above all, a uniting of all these themes with a pronounced interest in history and skill in the use of language, both oral and written. In all of his incarnations the soul that was eventually to become Sir Winston Spencer Churchill acted as if its personal destiny was indivisible from the destiny of the nation. It is the very artistry of destiny itself that Winston Churchill should have been the leader of the West in the battle between good and evil at the culmination of the first phase of the Apocalypse.

Another soul who was to become a great national leader in Europe in the twentieth century can be seen in a previous incarnation as Cardinal Richelieu of France. Here we see yet another man imbued with a sense of personal destiny which was inseparable from his personal mystical vision of the emerging grandeur of France. Nobody could have foretold that the tall, thin, pale boy, the third son of an insignificant upper-middle-class family, was to become the principal architect of France's greatness. Yet a discerning eye would have noted an inclination towards learning, a facility for debate and a relish for the prospect of governing the lives of others.

The young Richelieu saw the Church as a road to political power and by the age of twenty-two became a bishop, by Papal dispensation. By ensuring the appointment of prelates to the States General, he paved the way for his own rise to political power and his consequent appointment as

Cardinal. His supreme patriotism and visionary ideal of the absolute supremacy of Royal Authority led him repeatedly to place the interests of France before those of the Church. Though he lived in a time of bloody religious wars, he was a rationalist and pragmatist who regarded sin as civil disobedience and heresy as political dissension.

Richelieu was not universally popular and suffered a prolonged period of exile and banishment before he was recalled to the Royal Court and appointed Cardinal and First Minister of France. From the first days of his appointment he was the target of a series of conspiracies to remove him, but due to an excellent intelligence system which he himself created, he was always able to remain in power. He steered France through the Thirty Years War during which he displayed unsuspected gifts of generalship. After the successful siege of la Rochelle he personally led his army on a forced march across the Alps in midwinter to defeat the unsuspecting Spaniards who threatened his southern flank.

At the end of his career he had made possible the grandeur of France by ensuring the military eclipse of Spain and the Habsburg hegemony. He had laid the foundations of the French Empire in North Africa by establishing strong economic links with Morocco. He is also remembered for founding the French Academy. His accumulation of wealth was considered excessive even by the standards of the age but his money was largely dedicated to the patronage of the arts and to the endowment of the Sorbonne where he was finally buried.

Nobody, not even his own father, could ever have conceived that the five-year-old boy, to whom playing with soldiers had become an obsession, was the reincarnation of Cardinal Richelieu. It was only after he had attended the military academy of St Cyr, fought heroically at Verdun and joined the French Supreme War Council that Charles de Gaulle began to be recognized for his revolutionary and controversial ideas on the art of modern war. His book *The Army of the Future*, which advocated a small, professional, highly mobile army as opposed to the static defensive system of the Maginot Line, made him unpopular with his military superiors, especially Marshal Petain who had once been the commanding officer of his infantry regiment. Tragically it was the Panzer Generals, Guderian and Rommel, of the German *Wehrmacht* who implemented his ideas on mobile warfare and used them to bring about the defeat of the French army.

When Marshal Petain started negotiations for an armistice with the Germans, Charles de Gaulle, Secretary of Defence in Reynaud's government, departed for England to continue the struggle to free France. His historic broadcasts from London to all true patriots were the rallying cry to fight on and regain the very soul of France. In his absence, he was court-martialled, sentenced to death and all his property confiscated.

Believing totally that he was a man of destiny whose mission was to save France, the then almost unknown de Gaulle with grudging support from the British Government founded the Free French Forces and acted as a *de facto* government in exile. Moving his HQ to Algeria in 1943, where he increased the size of his armies, he prepared for the liberation of France. He arrived in Paris within hours of the liberation of the city, and despite great personal risk insisted on attending a mass of thanksgiving at Notre Dame. His main concerns at this time were to establish a government free from communist influence and to secure for France her rightful place at the negotiating table at the end of the war.

After two short periods in provisional government he unpredictably resigned from office in anger and disappointment with all the political parties forming the coalition. He founded the RPF, a national movement, which rapidly developed into a political party which gained 120 seats in the national assembly. Disgusted with the machinations of the politicians of the Fourth Republic, he again resigned, returning to the village of Colombey les Deux Églises to write his memoirs and await the call from the people of France that he knew would inevitably come. His public statements that he was 'the man whose destiny was to restore France to her former glory', evoked international derision abroad and political indifference and disdain from most of the population of France.

The dramatic call to duty came in 1958 at a time when France was faced with the possibility of civil war over the continuing chaos of the Algerian insurrection. Called to power by what was virtually a military junta, he refused to take office by any other than legal means. Installed as Prime Minister to save Algeria for the French, he used public support to save France – by ending her rule in Algeria – a move which endeared him to the majority of the French people, but disgusted many of the military who had brought him to power. This controversial act, viewed as an act of total betrayal by the Generals, brought about a mutiny in the army which led to a vicious and bitter civil war in which disaffected army officers created the OAS, or secret army, dedicated to the overthrow of de Gaulle, by now President of France.

At this point in de Gaulle's career we can see the strongest parallel in his remarkably similar destiny to Cardinal Richelieu who also faced insurrection and became a target for assassination. De Gaulle protected himself by using the modern development of the very intelligence services which originated with Richelieu. It was Richelieu who was instrumental in bringing French influence into North Africa and de Gaulle who ended it, both acting for the good of France.

Like Richelieu, de Gaulle was entirely motivated by his

concept of the grandeur of France, based on order and stability. The founding of the Fifth Republic and the acceptance of its constitution by public referendum effectively bypassed all political opposition and allowed de Gaulle the freedom to achieve the economic and political restructuring of France. Just as Richelieu was prepared to ignore his allegiance to the Catholic Church if it served the interests of France, so de Gaulle was also ready to sacrifice strongly held opinions and long-term associates in order to promote the grandeur of France as he saw it.

At the conclusion of both their illustrious careers, these strong-willed and stubborn men, two similar beads on a single thread, left France as a strong, self-sufficient and independent nation. Richelieu relieved France from the threat of the Habsburg Alliance and de Gaulle divorced the nation from the unpopular political influence of the USA and the military interference of the NATO Alliance.

It may seem surprising that a prelate like Richelieu should return to earth as a General but, apart from the fact that Cardinal Richelieu was himself skilled in war, most of the Chiefs of General Staff on all sides in both World Wars had lived former lives either as Popes or Cardinals. And this even includes the Turkish Army Commander, Kemal Ataturk, who had formerly been Pope Alexander, the Borgia Pope. In this respect the former incarnations of the German High Command as a succession of Popes in the ninth century, were dealt with fully in Part One of *The Spear of Destiny*. Even Adolf Hitler himself in one of his earlier lives on earth had appeared as the Archbishop of Capua of the same historical period.

The earliest known incarnation of Adolf Hitler is the figure of Ahab in the Old Testament, the black magician who, together with his wife Jezebel, worshipped the god Baal and plotted the murder of the prophet Elijah. We next find him in the person of Herod the Great, an Arab who with Roman help fought his way from obscurity to become the King of Israel. It was the same Herod who ordered the slaughter of the innocents in an attempt to kill the infant Jesus. This episode on which his popular notoriety rests is in fact out of character with the historical reality of a brave and resourceful king, builder and administrator, who brought order and stability to the area now known as the Near East. It was Herod who completely rebuilt the Temple in Jerusalem, founded the port of Caesarea, and built fortresses as far south as the Jordan and as far north as Damascus. He was a friend of Pompey, Julius Caesar and Mark Antony, for whom he built the Antonia which became the permanent residence of the Roman Proconsuls including Pontius Pilate. Towards the end of his life, however, he developed a cruel and violent streak which undermined his whole character.

Herod was a Jew in name only, and it is his Arab origins which led to his next appearance at the time of the advent of Islam, an incarnation which later influences Hitler in his prophetic vision and his urge towards world conquest. Nuremberg, where Hitler held his great Aryan blood rallies, for good reason became known universally as the 'Mecca' of the Nazi Party. The next bead on the thread of this spiritual biography was the Landulf of Capua, the historical figure behind the black magician Klingsor in the Grail sagas and Wagner's opera *Parsifal*. It was the Landulf who sought by evil means to destroy the Grail impulse while at the same time plotting with the Arabs to bring about the Islamic occupation of Europe. (Again this has been fully dealt with in the earlier book.)

One of the least suspected incarnations of Adolf Hitler was the person of Philip II of Spain, the most powerful man in Europe in his time who was responsible for sending the Armada to invade Britain. Like Herod the Great, King

Philip of Spain presided over his country at the time of its greatest development, in both cases immediately prior to its sudden decline. Philip was responsible for the building of the monumental and imposing palace of the Escorial, from which he ruled his empire autocratically by decree, distrusting all his advisers and insisting on minutely detailed reports on all matters of importance. Administration was slow and difficult as, from time to time, he prevaricated on decisions, and left their implementation to his corrupt and ill-chosen courtiers. Philip once stated he would rather give up all his empire than rule over heretics, and he fought against heresy as if it were the worst sort of treason. The record of the Spanish Inquisition at this time is well known.

While most of the leading characters in history seem to be motivated by the more positive and virtuous themes of their previous lives, Adolf Hitler appears to have incorporated in one lifetime every negative aspect from all his previous incarnations. The only continuing beneficial trait to come through was his love of architecture on an epic scale, but even this was made to serve his racist doctrines and his ambition for world conquest.

The Nazi clique which surrounded Hitler bore a startling resemblance to the ring of courtiers around Philip II, as did Hitler's attitude to them in which he mirrored Philip's suspicion and pathological distrust of his advisers – 'His dagger was always close to his smile', records one of his biographers, again similar to the pervasive fear that existed in the circle of Nazi élite who served the Führer of the Third Reich. The man who spoke of himself as 'possessed' – 'I go like a sleepwalker where providence dictates' – and chose to become the manifestation of the first appearance of the Leviathan, was not unnaturally surrounded by demonically inspired minions who continued their former roles in the Inquisition, but on this occasion carried them further into the immensity of evil known as the Holocaust.

*　*　*

It is not only one pattern of history that is being repeated and developed in any given period. For instance in the North African desert the battle between Hannibal and the Roman General Scipio Africanus was refought between the armies of General Rommel and Montgomery of Alamein. General Patton, who is well known to have believed in reincarnation, was himself the rebirth of Hasdrubal the brother of Hannibal, and this is why destiny did not allow a military confrontation between Patton and Rommel. Whilst on the other side of the world General Douglas MacArthur, a reborn Shinto Emperor, led the American forces in the war in the Pacific and accepted the Japanese surrender. Of course, it is not only the great leaders who reappear; also incarnating around them are all those thousands of souls with whom they were connected in their previous lives. It is in this way that the drama and symbolism of history is the transformation of the lives and events of previous ages.

Fortunately the drama and symbolism of history and destiny itself are not exclusively concerned with statesmen, tyrants and Generals. In the development of human destiny it is arguable that perhaps the greatest contributory personalities have been the philosophers, creative artists, writers and scientists as well as the great spiritual leaders throughout the ages.

Eastern systems of philosophy see life on earth as a wheel of suffering from incarnation to incarnation, and the only salvation as escape from it. The western school, exemplified by the German philosopher Lessing in his *Education of the Human Race*, perceives the whole process of reincarnation as a continuing school of development in which every human experiences each sequential step in the overall evolution of human consciousness. In such a manner each individual, every time he touches the historical process, can not only make good his past errors and fulfil his own personal destiny, but at the same time contribute lovingly to the overall spiritual development of mankind – and in this way the Karma of the family, the nation and the aims of the spirit of the time are fulfilled.

Plato was the first western philosopher to describe the process of reincarnation as a means of balancing the scales of justice from life to life. Some of the early church fathers like Origen and Ammonius Saccas considered reincarnation to be part of the Christian doctrine but all such ideas were put aside by St Augustine of Hippo who insisted that the human soul was created when the child took its first breath. Pelagius, an antagonist of Augustine, spoke of the prenatal existence of the soul. And it is Pelagius who later returns to earth as Traherne, the poet whom we quoted in this respect regarding the path to unveiling the meaning of personal destiny. Above all it was the Manichaean stream who saw reincarnation as providing a possibility of redemption from the sins of former lives which could be made good again.

The members of any school of philosophy reappear again together. Examples of this are the return of the Platonists as the so-called Platonic Fathers of Chartres, Plato himself returning as Bernardus, and Socrates in the figure of Fulbertus (who later reappeared in more modern times as Tolstoy). While the Aristotelians reappear as the great scholastics of the Dominican Order around St Thomas Aquinas, who was the rebirth of Aristotle himself.

Except in rare instances of the isolated appearance of a startling genius like Shakespeare who was the reappearance of Aeschylus, the greatest tragedian of ancient Greece, or Dante who was inspired by a previous life as Sophocles, most of the great artists also reincarnate as associates from previous lives on earth. This becomes most obvious at the time of the Italian Renaissance where many of the great geniuses received their early training in Florence. They reappear two centuries later in the wave of classical

116

composers of whom Mozart is a prime example.

Mozart, an infant prodigy whose very genius appeared effortless, had previously lived as Michelangelo, one of the greatest sculptors and painters of all time, who gave us not only the carvings of Moses, David, and the Pietàs, but also the magnificent painting of the Last Judgement on the ceiling of the Sistine Chapel. Michelangelo, with good reason, painted his own face in the portrayal of the martyrdom of the Apostle Bartholomew. A previous life of St Bartholomew had been Marsyas, the ancient Greek who refused to play his flute to the gods. As Mozart, he composed *The Magic Flute*, an opera which thinly veils the path of initiation and for this disclosure the famous composer was reputedly poisoned by some of the Freemasons of Vienna who considered him to have betrayed their mysteries.

The entire process of reincarnation cannot be seen in its true perspective unless it is projected against the whole background of the evolution of human consciousness. It is in this context that the repeating lives of great religious figures can be more fully understood. Figures such as Arjuna who in the *Bhagavad Gita* is depicted as holding a dialogue with the sun god Krishna regarding his quandary over making war on his own blood relatives. Arjuna reappears in the personality of St Paul who on the road to Damascus is blinded by his vision of the risen Christ which brings to him the conviction that the old covenant based on the blood of the Jewish race has been replaced by universal love.

The disciples of Buddha reappear on earth as the founders of the Franciscan Order. Buddhism taught that the earth was 'Maya' or worthless illusion and that life on earth was merely involvement in a wheel of suffering, but now as Christian friars, though they wear simple robes and still carry their begging bowls, they find human life meaningful and recognize nature as a living part of God's creation. Asita, one of Gautama's closest disciples, is reborn as the soul we know as St Francis of Assisi. Once again he follows the path of love, but now inspired by Christ he is the first Christian saint who discovers man's spiritual unity with nature.

It will be fruitful for our understanding of the meaningfulness of repeated earthly lives, if we follow the spiritual biography of one of the leading Greek philosophers of that ancient time when atavistic picture consciousness was receding to be replaced by conscious thinking. A leading figure in this transition is Empedocles (490 BC) in whose soul the two contrasting modes of conception clashed violently. Empedocles could not bear to be deprived of a natural unity with nature and his whole philosophy is a revolt against the extirpation of the spiritual reality of nature. He felt that the intellect had exiled him from his natural spiritual inheritance. His extraordinary motive when he committed suicide, by throwing himself into the crater of Mount Etna, was to experience for but a brief second the working of creative forces within the volatile elements which consumed him. He reappears as perhaps the greatest painter of the Italian Renaissance, Leonardo da Vinci, who combines in himself both the paradigm of the ancient mysteries and the seed of the modern scientific conception; a man who could paint *The Last Supper* in which Christ as the King of the Elements consecrates the bread and the wine, and at the same time display scientific genius in his mastery of anatomical drawing, conception of flight, the submarine and designs for a form of gyrocompass – the development of which is used in modern space rockets. If you held the remnants of the writings of Empedocles about nature in one hand and the notebooks of Leonardo in the other, you would be impressed both by the similarity of their observations of nature and by their conclusions.

Adolph Hitler (Imperial War Museum).

Winston Spencer Churchhill at the
door of number 10 Downing Street
(Imperial War Museum).

President F. D. Roosevelt signing the declaration of war with Japan, wearing
a black armband in mourning for Pearl Harbor (Imperial War Museum).

'Le Grand Charles'
General Charles de Gaulle,
President of France and the
reincarnation of Cardinal
Richelieau.

General 'Blood and Guts'
Patton. The only American
military leader to recognize
the true significance of The
Spear of Destiny
(Imperial War Museum).

The Imperial Crown, Apple, Sceptre, Crosses, the Imperial Sword, and the Sword of St. Maurice. These items of the Imperial Regalia known collectively as the 'Reichkleinodien' are on view in the Treasure House in the Hofburg in Vienna. The Sword of St. Maurice was later mistaken by the Nazis for the Spear of Longinus [seen below] (Kunsthistoriches Museum, Vienna).

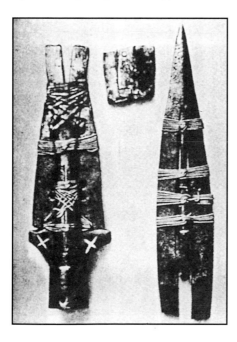

The Spear of Longinus, often named the Maurice Spear, now consists of two parts held together by a silver sheath. A nail from the Cross of Christ has been inserted into the blade and is held in place by gold, silver, and copper threads. The base of the spearhead is embossed with gold crosses.

General view of Hiroshima after the Atomic bombing (Imperial War Museum).

The wreckage of Managua after the Nicaraguan earthquake of 1972 (Popperfoto).

The eruption of Mount St. Helens on October 22, 1986—general view of the plume of steam and ash (Popperfoto).

Rosslyn Chapel, exterior, South side (Michael Green).

The Pretence Pillar, Rosslyn Chapel
(Michael Green).

The Master Mason's Pillar, Rosslyn
Chapel (Michael Green).

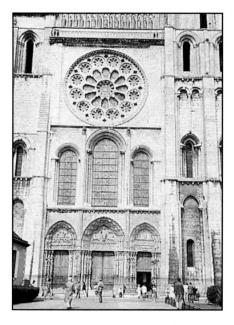

The triple doors that form the main entrance to Chartres Cathedral
(Tim Wallace-Murphy).

Detailed and loving carving of the last judgement, over the side entrance. Carved 'Ad Majorem Dei Gloriam' by the anonymous masons who built Chartres Cathedral
(Tim Wallace-Murphy).

The Christian version of 'Virginibus Parituras'. The carving of the Blessed Virgin Mary over the portal of Chartres Cathedral (Tim Wallace-Murphy).

Christ the King, immortalized in stone over the main door of Chartres Cathedral (Tim Wallace-Murphy).

In this period of the great change in paradigm, Leonardo was chosen to return almost immediately to earth in the figure of Giordano Bruno, philosopher, scientist and occultist whose theories more than any other soul of that age anticipated modern science. Bruno was the first to conceive of other solar systems in which his thinking reached beyond Copernicus who still conceived of a finite universe with fixed stars. Above all, Bruno worked on the relationship between the individual soul and the universal soul of nature. He began his career as a priest in the Dominican Order but quickly turned towards teaching philosophy in which he held tenaciously to unorthodox ideas which resulted in seven years' imprisonment and torture at the hands of the Inquisition, and finally led to his death at the stake for heresy.

The genius in the thread of spiritual biography which emerged like beads in the form of Empedocles, Leonardo and Giordano Bruno finally reappeared in the renowned German poet, Johann Wolfgang Goethe. This poetic genius who is mainly remembered for *Faust* was also responsible for building the bridge back towards man's reunion with nature. Goethe felt an inner certainty that the same path of scientific knowledge which was bringing man down into the seeming impasse of materialism, also held the key to a reascent into a far more penetrating and spiritual vision of nature. He found a way through which thinking and perception could be raised to a level of higher consciousness so that it would pass the bounds of sense existence and arrive at an objective understanding of the spiritual background of the natural world. He achieved a new clairvoyant perception by introducing into it a quality of imagination which he called 'extra-percipient fantasy', and in doing this he laid the foundation for what is now called the holistic approach to science, which contains within it the answers to many of the problems of the modern age.

* * *

119

It would be pointless to reveal list after list of the reincarnations of leading personalities in history, or how entire peoples reincarnate in new locations and into the blood of different races, as for instance the way in which the tribes of ancient Huns incarnated into Japan or the Magyars into Korea. Our intention within the context of this book was to give a few examples to show the working of the artistry of human destiny. Enough, we hope, to show that without the working of reincarnation patterns, the drama and symbolism of history would be merely meaningless coincidence. For what would it mean for the human soul if it only touched the whole evolution of humanity at but one point as a slave in ancient Egypt, a feudal serf, or a factory hand in New Jersey, the Ruhr or Manchester?

Above all we have attempted to demonstrate how history is in the widest sense a very personal affair and that the entire contemporary world is still fast asleep to the real meaning of the historical process. The history of the present time is something that we have helped to create in our former lives on earth. We bear the whole responsibility for what the world was, what it is, and what it will become. By changing our own lives out of this realization we can start to transform the world in which we live. Only if we face this responsibility with courage can we understand the real meaning of human destiny and be able to perceive the face of the Apocalypse in the unfolding decades of our own time.

SECTION 3

THE SEEDS OF TERROR

They Know Not What They Do!
Atomic Physics, 666–1945

for whatsoever a man soweth,
that shall he also reap.
The Epistle to the Galatians (King James Version): 6:7

No new impulse or invention arises by accident or coincidence – the seeds were sown in previous incarnations by those involved; this is especially true in the case of the invention of the atomic bomb. The seeds of atomic physics did not arise in Cambridge or Göttingen, but long ago in a forgotten academy lying beneath the Afghan foothills in ancient Persia.

Whole communities of people working together in one incarnation are led by destiny to continue their work together in the next. Successive incarnations of such groups can often create, for good or evil, critical events in history.

Evil powers utilize the process of reincarnation and the working of Karma to sow the seeds of destruction which reach across the millennia in an attempt to dominate or destroy mankind. These evil powers can even seduce people with the best intent as happened with the creators of the atomic bomb, who were inspired to develop this horrendous weapon in a race against the evil tide of the Hitler regime.

Only later, when they perceived how they had been the pawns of fate, did they realize they were working in 'the Service of the Devil'.

CHAPTER TEN

THE ACADEMY OF HADES, 'THE NUMBER OF THE BEAST IS 666'

Because of yesterday, has tomorrow been cancelled?

History is a very personal affair!

The entire contemporary world is fast asleep to the real meaning of the historical process. People blame everybody else but themselves for the disastrous situation the whole world is confronting. What people refuse to recognize is that they themselves have helped to create the contemporary world situation by their deeds in former lives. They themselves, as a result of their thoughts, words and deeds in earlier lives on earth, have created the world situation into which they are born. We must all bear the total responsibility for the situation that the world is in today.

Now that you have come to understand something regarding the drama and symbolism of history as the result of the interweaving of personal reincarnation patterns, you may have enough insight to understand how the seed of the atomic age under the shadow of the Pale Horse was first planted more than fourteen hundred years ago.

The immediate question is where did this take place and who were the people most immediately involved in planting the seeds for the emergence of the present international situation in which the whole world faces the threat of instant extinction. In answering these two questions, and revealing the previous lives of the leading atomic scientists, we will unveil the nature and the significance of the apocalyptic Beast whose number is 666.

Of course, purely rational and unperceptive thinking will insist that there is absolutely no difference between atomic physics and any other aspect of science. But we have illustrated how physical nature has two borders, one touching the realm of intramaterial energies which are liberated by disrupting the structure of atomic nuclei, the other leading over into creative chaos, the chalice of all that appears in intelligent design, the border through which creative forces fashion, sustain, and inform the living forms in the terrestrial world.

The leading atomic physicists of the twentieth century have an entirely different Karmic reincarnation pattern to all other souls. They were incarnate together in a succession of generations in the sixth, seventh and eighth centuries AD at the Academy of Jundi-Shapur in Persia. How this tremendously significant academy came to be founded in this period is one of the most mysterious happenings of history. On the face of it, the Academy of Jundi-Shapur seems to have arisen out of a whole series of coincidences, but any sensitive historian with genuine insight cannot but feel the presence of evil forces working in from another dimension.

The first event in this chain of coincidences happened in AD 489 when Zeno Isauricus closed the famous school in Edessa and expelled its Nestorian scholars from his territories. The Bishop of Edessa had earlier named them as heretics. Now all these scholars became migrants in the Arab lands of the Middle East. The unforeseen and unintended result of Byzantine Christian intolerance finally forced these wandering scholars to congregate in Persia. The next significant event happened when the Emperor Justinian, an ecclesiastical bigot, prohibited the functioning of the Greek schools of philosophy within his vast empire. These schools were indeed the shining light of antiquity. All the great scholarship of olden times which had been drawn into the Greek schools of philosophy, and had produced an Anaxagorus, a Heraclitus, and later a Socrates, a Plato and an Aristotle, were now swept away into oblivion by a sudden decree in AD 529. It is certainly possible to gain some idea why Justinian out of dogmatism wished to sweep away all the pre-Christian knowledge of ancient Greece; but if we reflect honestly on these matters we must remain dissatisfied with any of the explanations which recorded history gives us. We sense behind all these expulsions of the scholars the direct weaving of powerful forces of evil.

The exiled Greek philosophers journeyed to Persia where they were received by the enlightened and wisdom-loving King Khusraw Anusharwan who set up an Academy for them in Jundi-Shapur. Here they were joined by the exiled Nestorians and by a large group of industrious and assimilative Syrians, who made up in diligence what they lacked in originality. King Anusharwan was a great admirer of Greek culture and especially wished to introduce Greek science into his dominions. It was his intention to have in Persia a Greek academy of the same high quality and reputation as the great Greek Academy in Alexandria. In Jundi-Shapur beneath the mountains of Afghanistan the Academy was instituted and at first the Alexandrian curriculum was introduced, and books and manuscripts including the medical works of Galen were studied and lectured upon as at Alexandria. The King sent his own personal physician, Burzuya, to India, and he brought back works on Indian medicine and a group of Indian physicians. Many other emissaries brought Greek scholars from Alexandria and sages from all over the territories of Asia Minor.

It was in the Academy itself in Jundi-Shapur that the works of Aristotle were translated. And the remarkable thing is that Aristotle, whose works might otherwise have been completely lost, had been first translated into Syrian at Edessa, by those very men who had been driven out by

Zeno Isauricus. This Syrian translation was brought to Jundi-Shapur, and there translated into Arabic. Thus it came about that the Aristotelian concepts were imbued with Arabian light, thrown over them by the remarkable souls of the Arabians of that time, in whom the keenest thinking was united with a certain visionary capacity – a visionary capacity, however, which took its course on logical lines and then rose to actual spirit perception. Thus it was, in the light of this characteristic teaching, that an impressive and highly significant world outlook developed in Jundi-Shapur during the seventh century.

Although it was extraordinary enough that such an Academy was so quickly established, funded and maintained in such a short period of time – an Academy encompassing so many brilliant minds from all quarters of the civilized world, its real significance arose from the planned activities of one particular family, the family of Ben Jesu who had the very highest reputation as physicians and who are recorded as the leaders of this international community over several generations.

Before we can understand the sinister motives of Joshua Ben Jesu who actually founded the Academy and personally set up its curriculum, we must take a brief look at what was happening in the evolution of human consciousness in this period. The brief age of enlightenment brought about by the appearance of the great Church Fathers was over. The Roman Church had swept away all the ancient knowledge of the spiritual world, the established procedures of initiation and the pagan temples and oracles. All inquiries into the condition of the soul before birth had been eradicated by St Augustine of Hippo who proclaimed that the human soul was created at the moment of the first breath of life. The idea of reincarnation had become a heresy. The earth and the whole of nature were looked upon as Godless and involved in the fall from paradise. The great Greek

125

Mystery Temples were defunct and the oracles silent. The great heretic and Caesar Julian, the Apostate, had been the very last to attain initiation into the spiritual world through the three-day 'Temple Sleep' of the Elysian Mysteries. Amongst intellectuals of this period, the spirit senses had already atrophied; only the unthinking peasants in the civilized territories and the migrating tribes from the north still had a vestige of the old atavistic vision. At no time in the whole historical process was mankind more blind to the realities of the spiritual world. Meanwhile the Roman Empire in the west was in a state of decline and the Eastern Byzantine Empire was defending itself with difficulty against the onslaught of the tribes pouring southwards.

It was in this milieu that Joshua Ben Jesu was demonically inspired to set up the Academy of Jundi-Shapur. The Ben Jesu family and its immediate circle of associates had been rightfully exiled by the Nestorian Church for developing an unnatural form of clairvoyance through black magic. Unlike the physical eye which develops according to the laws of nature to perceive the natural world and is approximately similar in every human being, the clairvoyant 'eye' is a result of personal development along a chosen spiritual path and its perception is conditioned by the moral motivation of the adept. That is to say that the nature of clairvoyant perception itself and the spiritual beings and realities which it perceives differ greatly from one initiation school to another, especially so when black magic techniques are used which reveal only an evil perspective. The Ben Jesu family secretly perceived the god Behemoth and their motive was to replace Christianity with the worship of this mighty evil being who was none other than Sorat, the two-horned beast of the Apocalypse. 'This calls for wisdom', says St John in the Revelation (New International Version): 13, verse 8. 'If anyone has insight, let him calculate the number of the beast, for it is man's number. His number is 666.'

126

The Academy of Jundi-Shapur, outwardly a Christian Academy but in nothing else but name, began to fulfil its sinister aim in the year AD 666. This will not be the only time that we show how St John in the Revelation prophesied with accuracy dates and circumstances which are now a matter of historical record.

On the face of it the curriculum included subjects which were not in any way abnormal for this period of history – mathematics, astronomy, medicine and philosophy. It was the method of teaching that was unique in the entire history of mankind. By methods of meditation, mantras, and magic the students were prepared in a unique discipline for the actual vision of Behemoth. And it was Behemoth, or as we have called him, Ahriman, who taught them personally in their ecstatic condition, science in a very advanced and sophisticated form.

The teaching in Jundi-Shapur shows the greatest imaginable contrast to everything that was planned for in the rightful evolution of consciousness. The students were required only to prepare themselves for the clairvoyant vision of Behemoth. After that his all-embracing wisdom poured into them with immediacy to bring about an instinctive form of genius for which no effort of their own was required. But, of course, the clairvoyance of the students did not give them a perception of the spiritual world. Instead they were deluged with knowledge about man and the physical universe which they were taught to consider as self-sufficient in itself. It was a phenomenon of the greatest power, an intoxicating experience, and a teaching in the highest sense dangerous to the real future of mankind. This way of knowledge was meant to spread across the whole civilized world. It is hardly possible today to picture what course history would have taken if the motives of Ahriman had been fulfilled at that time. Man would certainly have acquired an unripe knowledge of himself and nature out of a kind of instinct – but the instinct of genius. Men would have been overwhelmed by this knowledge, disabled by it, and their whole future evolution cut short.

If the Academy of Jundi-Shapur had not been brought by a surprising source to an abrupt and bloody end, the whole civilized world would have been transformed by its influence. For even before the year AD 1000 man would already have had all the scientific advances which have been realized in our own time, like the petrol engine, electromagnetic power, psychology, brain-washing techniques, instant communication, data storage and retrieval systems, rocketry and atomic physics! Just imagine what would have happened to mankind at this period in history if they had already mastered what we call today 'Modern Science'.

And beyond this, man would have become a kind of automaton. For the central philosophical teaching given by Behemoth in Jundi-Shapur about man himself was aimed at removing the value of all personal moral development. Just imagine this circle of exiled sages and their associates from all over the then known world absorbing in ecstatic immediacy the teachings of the being the Revelation calls the Beast of 666, the wisdom of terrestrial man isolated for ever from the gods. 'When a man dies,' taught Behemoth, 'it is only the substance of his psyche which flows back into the universe. Man himself has no personal individuality; all that is psyche is merely a reflection of the universal psyche.' So taught the two-horned beast whom the Revelation predicts will actually incarnate on this planet in our time in flesh and blood and deluge mankind with his technological genius and terrestrial magic, to lead them into the hands of the second appearance of the Leviathan, the Great Dictator of the coming world power.

The present town of Jundi-Shapur has been built on another site. Approximately ten miles north-west of Tustar on the road to Dizful, I discovered the ruins of the ancient

Academy in a place now called Sharabad. The original city of Jundi-Shapur, where the Academy was later established, was founded by a Persian King, Shapur I (AD 224–241). From a cave in the mountains above where this city was later set, the original Zarathustra gave out his teachings regarding the Sun God and how the souls of human beings on earth were involved in the struggle between the Light of Ormuzd and the Darkness of Ahriman. Here too in this very city Mani was martyred and skinned alive as a result of his significant initiation teachings in which he considered man to have been created to redeem the evil in the universe.

In the evening light which shone on the ruins of the great Academy like a sword blade I could experience the echoes of the battle between darkness and light which had taken place there. It was a powerful experience to stand in the very place where the Beast of 666 once sought to take over the whole earth. I could still feel the last echo of the mighty, dark intelligence which poured into the students like an inoculation of knowledge, a kind of technological magic which they received effortlessly as an instant revelation. It seemed imperative to trace where these souls would reincarnate again and how their reappearance would affect the entire destiny of mankind. Especially the Ben Jesu family and their immediate associates amongst the Nestorian exiles who had taken over complete control of the Academy.

Had the plan of Behemoth worked in Jundi-Shapur as he had intended, we should not be writing AD 1990 today but 1990 minus 666, or 1324; for Behemoth would have inspired mankind in such a way that they would have regulated their chronology by him rather than by Jesus Christ. The aim of Behemoth was to make himself the god of the earth planet. In short, all the preliminaries to begin a new world religion were completed. 'Men will no longer direct their gaze to the spirit because the spirit will no longer interest them. I shall see to it that the individual human spirit will be abolished. [This he actually brought about through the great church council in AD 869.] Man will no longer consider himself an entelechy of body, soul and spirit but only body and soul because I shall relegate the human spirit to a mere intellectual quality in the psyche. No longer aware of his spirit, when man turns his attention to nature he will only form ghost-like concepts of it. Then I shall do something that men shall not notice, because they will not recognize themselves as real spiritual beings but merely as self-conscious material bodies. I shall gain complete control of their soul life. I shall lead man completely astray about his own nature while I pour into his intellect all the scientific discoveries which he would only achieve gradually in a much later epoch. Then I shall have humanity for myself – then I shall have caught them.'

The intention of the Beast was to cut man off from all further possibility of spiritual development. The atrophy of the spirit senses and the spiritual faculties would have become an irreversible process. Man would have had no opportunity to rediscover the spiritual world. Behemoth's plans for the Academy of Jundi-Shapur failed to materialize because of the sudden attack on the city itself. Completely, by surprise, the Academy was destroyed and most of its community put to death.

The onslaught came from retarded spiritual forces, which were nevertheless connected – though they also form a kind of opposition – with the onflow of the true Christian impulse. Through the sudden emergence of Mohammed and his visionary and fervently aggressive teaching, the whole effect of Jundi-Shapur was deadened. The ferocious Mohammedans, guided unwittingly by a higher power, drove northwards through Persia and, beneath the foothills of the Afghan mountains, reached the site of the Academy. At first the Academy defended itself with magical forces, putting out projections of supersensible demonic beings and even wild animals to frighten away the primitive tribesmen. But the fervour of Islam was too strong to be kept at bay. Finally the Academy was overrun and almost all of its inhabitants died by the sword. Only the hospital and its physicians, who could prove useful, were left untouched. And so it was that the devil looked after his own. The Ben Jesu family, the leading physicians of the Academy, were not only spared but allowed to continue their medical practice.

When Baghdad was founded in AD 762, the Caliph and his court became near neighbours of the surviving medical school in Jundi-Shapur and, before long, generous emoluments began to draw physicians from the remnant of the Academy. And in this Ja'far ibn Barmak, chief minister to Harun ar-Raschid, became the leading agent. But though he did everything in his power to introduce the wisdom of Jundi-Shapur amongst the subjects of the Caliph he failed to make it effective. Nevertheless the Nestorian heritage of Greek scholarship did pass from Athens and Edessa through Nisiblis to reappear in Baghdad after its sinister transformation in Jundi-Shapur. Mohammed's Islam had completely deadened the effect of the ghostly gnostic wisdom of the Academy, removing, as it were, the ground from under its feet. And here you can see the wisdom of the highest order in the drama and symbolism of world history. Indeed, we only come to know the truth about the advent of Mohammedanism when, in addition to other things, we know that the power of Islam was let loose on the world to deaden the power of the beast emanating from Jundi-Shapur. Although it did not stop the impulse from continuing to work right into our own time, it did take from it the strong Ahrimanically seductive force which would otherwise have been exercised almost immediately upon the whole of civilized mankind.

131

The Schoolmen of the Middle Ages knew they were fighting the demonic power of the Jundi-Shapur impulse which had escaped via Baghdad and entered Spain and England to spread across the continent of Europe. Albertus Magnus and Thomas Aquinas, the two great Dominicans, took up a quite definite attitude towards the Arabian philosophers of their time. See how in this sense in western Christian tradition the Schoolmen are shown with their Christian doctrine preparing to tread the Arabian men of learning underfoot. Over and over again in Christian art of the time we see the same passionate theme, the treading underfoot of the Arabian men of learning by the force of Christ. Study these pictures and you will understand how there lives in them the passionate wish of the Middle Ages to stand in opposition to all that originally sprang from the enmity of Jundi-Shapur towards Christ. All the passionate feeling against Arabian learning and its spreading across the European continent right up to the time of Averroës, Maimonides Rambam and Avicenna is expressed in the Christian art of this period. Only study it for yourself and you will see the last echo of all that we have been describing.

What is it today that still remains with us from the remnants of Behemoth's knowledge which escaped from Jundi-Shapur via Baghdad? Believe it or not, it is western scientific thinking! The so-called impartial materialistic thinking of today. The very type of thinking which has obliterated moral conscience from scientific inquiry and has brought mankind to the brink of destruction in the twentieth century.

All the teachers and pupils involved in the community of the academy in Jundi-Shapur have reincarnated or will soon reincarnate once more in this century. Who are they? And where can we find them? They are the leading atomic physicists! Their new Jundi-Shapur was the research facility of Los Alamos in New Mexico which became the international meeting place for all the atomic physicists who were concerned in creating the atom bomb and who are now leading mankind into the space age. And what of Behemoth? This time he will actually incarnate amongst his pupils in a physical body of flesh and blood. He will be the progeny of the reincarnating generations of the Ben Jesu family who set up Jundi-Shapur as a vessel for his teaching. He is the Anti-Christ of the Revelation − the two-horned beast of the Apocalypse.

CHAPTER ELEVEN

THE SPEAR AND THE KARMA OF THE ATOM BOMB

I am become Death, the shatterer of worlds.

The United States of America became the new claimants to the Spear of Destiny at 2.10 pm on 30 April 1945. This was the moment when Adolf Hitler shot himself in the bunker beneath the ruins of the Reich Chancellery in Berlin. It was also the moment when US army intelligence, section five, discovered the Spear hidden in a vault beneath Nuremberg Castle.

On the brilliant, sunny afternoon of that fateful April day a party of GIs began searching the ruins of the *Oberen Schmied Gasse* below the towering fortress of Nuremberg which had now become the American Seventh Army Headquarters. It is not recorded whether these troops were on official duty flushing out SS still hiding in basements throughout the city which had been reduced to rubble, or whether on their own account they were hunting for loot and liquor, often hidden away in the cellars of demolished houses.

One of these men found himself peering down through a pile of rubble at the back of a garage into a wide tunnel which apparently stretched far into the murky darkness beneath the precipitous cliff. Calling his companions, who unslung their weapons, he led them down by torchlight to the far end of the secret passage which terminated with two immense steel doors with both a lock and a dialling device. The soldiers knew immediately that whatever was behind these doors was of paramount importance. While two of the party stood guard at the entrance to the hidden bunker, the others ran off to report their astonishing find to Army HQ.

When the doors were opened it was found that the vault had its own generator and, when the lights and air conditioning system were switched on, a large chamber was revealed which was crammed full with Nazi loot stolen from countless European nations. Resting on top of an intricately carved, ten-foot-high altar from the historic church of St Mary in Krakow in Poland, stood an ancient leather case. Within the case, still resting on its faded red velvet dais, was the Spear of Longinus. The ancient weapon associated with the legend of world historic destiny had witnessed many scenes in its passage through two thousand years of history, but perhaps never so strange a setting as this secret underground vault which contained priceless antiquities, reliquaries, paintings, jewels and art treasures plundered from the many peoples whom the Nazis had subjugated during their short and brutal reign of power.

None of the American senators, who came to post-war Europe in droves, or the senior US Generals who made a special trip to Nuremberg to see this vast display of Nazi loot in the underground bunker in the Blacksmith's Alley, showed even the least interest in the age-old legend of the Spear of Longinus. The only exception was General 'Blood and Guts' Patton, one of the most colourful characters and perhaps one of the best Allied commanders of World War II.

General Patton, who had a historically orientated cast of mind, believed in reincarnation and had made a study of the quest for the Holy Grail, appears to have been totally fascinated at the sight of the Spear of Destiny. He took the ancient talisman of power from its leather case and removed the sleeve which holds the two separate parts of the spearhead together. He demanded the presence of local German historians to fill him in on the entire history of the ancient

Lance which was associated with the legend of world power. Aides scampered round to find the answers to his countless queries.

General Patton was the only American General who realized the true significance of the fact that the USA was now the official possessor of the Spear of Destiny. And he knew, too, the terrible significance of the imminent fulfilment of its legend once again. For the United States had discovered the secret of the manufacture of the atomic bomb, and the dropping of these fearsome weapons upon Japan was expected to bring an abrupt end to the war in the East.

To the veteran General, who still believed in the chivalry of war and would have preferred to have fought alongside Hannibal at Cannae than against Kesselring in the Ardennes, the atomic age meant the ending of an era in which the individual still had some significance. And while holding the talisman of power in his hands he told his aides that mankind was standing on the brink of the most evil epoch in the entire history of the planet. His young subordinates did not know about the atom bomb project which was still a most closely guarded secret at this time. They asked themselves what could be more evil than the concentration camps of Adolf Hitler's defeated regime, and they wondered if their General had finally 'gone off his head'.

General Patton left the bunker beneath the Nuremberg fortress in a sombre mood. Doom was written across the future of humanity unless human beings could live at peace with one another, and it was Patton above all who could see in all clarity the danger of the coming confrontation between America and Russia.

American soldiers were still standing guard outside the massive steel doors of the bunker under the *Oberen Schmied Gasse* in Blacksmith's Alley when American aircraft unleashed the first atom bombs on Hiroshima and Nagasaki. The Atomic Age had begun under the shadow of the Pale Horse whose rider is Death and whose following is the Hosts of Hell.

The Pale Horse whose presence was demonstrated with such vivid and appalling clarity when the *Enola Gay* dropped the first atom bomb on Japan, had gradually begun to emerge over the horizon of world history some years earlier in the aftermath of the First World War. We have already noted in an earlier chapter concerning the evolution of human consciousness that the transition from the age of the Black Horse to the emergence of the Pale Horse pointed to a further descent in the quality of thinking which passed beyond the realm of crass materialism into sub-human spheres – a thinking which has turned into cold inhuman abstraction in which human intelligence is in danger of becoming demonic. Strangely enough, it was in the 'beautiful days' of the flowering of university life in the twenties that, quite unnoticed, mankind was led across this sinister new threshold when physicists and mathematicians began to make a tremendous transformation of the scientific view of nature in the wake of Albert Einstein's new theory of relativity.

The pursuit of pure knowledge by a whole sequence of young geniuses in the totally abstract field of physics delved into a substratum of nature that appeared to be completely divorced from the realities of everyday life. The developments of mathematical formulae were pursued for their own sake and, in a completely abstract manner, the physicists were becoming more and more entranced by the complexities and beauty of the formulae they studied. They hoped to discover the secrets that would unveil the building blocks of ultimate reality, giving little thought to the eventual application for mankind of the investigations into the smallest portions of matter and how the nucleus of the atom could be artificially disintegrated.

It is not within our context to set down the history of theoretical physics. This is, in any case, well-known and its leading thinkers have to a large extent become household names. People like Rutherford working in Cambridge, Professor Niels Bohr in Copenhagen, the Joliot-Curies in Paris, Enrico Fermi in Italy, Max Planck, Felix Klein, Max Born, James Franck, David Hilbert from Göttingen, Arnold Sommerfeld from the University of Munich, and Otto Hahn and his partner Lise Meitner from Berlin. Göttingen was the epicentre of the intellectual activities of the physicists during the 'beautiful days' of the twenties. It became the focus for visiting physicists and students from all over Europe and the USA who were drawn into its orbit by the free flow of ideas and research reports published in the international journals of the time. These halcyon days gave rise to their unofficial motto *'Extra Gottingam non est vita'* (outside of Göttingen there is no life), which aptly demonstrates that they considered themselves to be the true leaders of society in the post-war years. Nobel prizes, honorary degrees, memberships of foreign scientific bodies seemed to be theirs by right in the old world peace of the Georgia Augusta University in Göttingen.

Among the brilliant community of international students who attended Göttingen was the American Robert J. Oppenheimer, who quickly became known as 'Oppy' and was greatly teased for his strange philosophical and literary tastes and particularly for his suggestion why Dante and his *Inferno* had located the eternal quest in hell instead of paradise. When Oppenheimer finally took his honours degree in May 1927, the man who was to become 'the father of the atom bomb' passed with distinction. Other young geniuses amongst the students were Werner Heisenberg, Leo Szilard and Edward Teller.

The beautiful days came to an abrupt end in 1933 when

Adolf Hitler came to power in Germany and the expulsion of the physicists began, mirroring the expulsion of the ancient Greek philosophers and sages from various parts of the Roman Empire in an earlier time. A large number of the exiled physicists were Jewish and had no alternative but to flee, the whole international community of physicists outside Germany coming to their assistance in finding new appointments. Many spent a short interim period in Copenhagen where Professor Niels Bohr gave them every facility to continue their work in his laboratories while, following the example of Einstein now securely ensconced in the Institute of Advanced Studies in Princeton, they applied for appointments throughout the major universities in America.

Many non-Jewish physicists also decided to leave as Hitler extended his hold first on Germany and later into Austria and Czechoslovakia. The Göttingen atomic physicists, like most other scientists throughout the world, behaved at first as though it were possible to ignore the Nazi political machine. Their very objectivity in the world of science prevented them from taking a strong stand over political issues. Gradually it became clear to them that interference from their new political masters was intolerable and completely inimical to their independence in matters of research, and their exodus began. There is a marked similarity between this exodus of scientists fleeing from political intolerance in Nazi Germany and the expulsion of the philosophers and sages from the Roman Empire in the reign of Justinian in the sixth century AD. And once again there was to be an immense and surprising change in their motives and their activities, the results of which were later called by no less a person than Bertrand Russell 'the service of the Devil'.

During these last few years before the advent of the Hitler War, theoretical physics was entering one of its most critical stages in which the nucleus of the atom was accidentally ruptured by the newly discovered neutrons, showing a potentiality for the release of immense energy. Only one scientist of note, the Nobel prize winner Walter Nernst, had some eighteen years earlier seen the dangers that lay ahead. 'We may say that we are living on an island of gun-cotton,' he said when he first read Rutherford's suggestion that the atom could be artificially disintegrated, 'but, thank God, we have not yet found the match that will ignite it.' As a result of the misuse of the powers of the Spear of Destiny which inspired Hitler in his attempt to gain world power, the search for the match began.

The Research Division of the German Army in Berlin held a special meeting in April 1939 to consider the possibility of a chain reaction in uranium. The German War Office became deeply interested, and immediately put an embargo on all exports of uranium ore from Czechoslovakia which the Third Reich had recently occupied. When this news reached America the exiled atomic physicists knew that the time had arrived to persuade the American Government to enter the race to make the atom bomb before such a weapon fell into the hands of Hitler.

Leo Szilard, formerly one of the leading minds in Göttingen, made a visit to Albert Einstein with the intention of persuading him to write a letter which would draw the attention of the American Government to the threat of the German manufacture of an atom bomb. Accompanying Szilard was Edward Teller who translated into English Einstein's statement. Einstein, who had no very clear idea of what was happening in nuclear physics, signed the document. It gave the unknown Szilard an aura of authority and credibility. However, it was not a physicist but an international financier who approached Roosevelt to present the case.

Although Roosevelt regarded Alexander Sachs as a man of great ability with a real passion for anonymity he was not immediately persuaded to take action. Yet he agreed to see the banker for another session at breakfast the next morning, when the influential financier found the President sitting alone at the table in his wheelchair.

'What bright idea have you got now? How much time would you like to explain it?'

Dr Sachs says he replied that he would not take long.

'All I want to do is to tell you a story. During the Napoleonic wars a young American inventor came to the French Emperor and offered to build a fleet of steamships with the help of which Napoleon could, in spite of the uncertain weather, land in England. Ships without sails? This seemed to the great Corsican so impossible that he sent Fulton away. In the opinion of the English historian Lord Acton, this is an example of how England was saved by the short-sightedness of an adversary. Had Napoleon shown more imagination and humility at that time, the history of the nineteenth century would have taken a very different course.'

After Sachs finished speaking the President remained silent for several minutes. Roosevelt ... [sent for] a bottle of old French brandy of Napoleon's time, which the Roosevelt family had possessed for many years. The President, still maintaining a significant silence, told [a servant] to fill two glasses. Then he raised his own, nodded to Sachs, and drank to him.

Next he remarked: 'Alex, what you are after is to see that the Nazis don't blow us up?'

'Precisely.'

It was only then that Roosevelt called in his attaché, General 'Pa' Watson, and addressed him – pointing to the document Sachs had brought – in words which have since become famous: 'Pa, this requires action!'

Brighter Than a Thousand Suns: Robert Jungk, pp. 106–7

Despite Roosevelt's manifest interest in the project no funds were available from the government for atomic research and the military authorities showed little or no interest. Even a second letter from Einstein in March 1940, regarding the intensification of German interest in uranium since the beginning of the war, did not help. Characteristically, the American authorities did not awaken to the realities until the British, who were clearly making progress, declared that it seemed 'quite probable that the atom bomb may be manufactured before the end of the war'. As destiny would have it, exactly one day before the Japanese attack on Pearl Harbor, which precipitated America into the global conflict, the long-delayed decision was taken to give enormous financial and technical backing for an earnest attempt to construct the new weapon. It was not long before some 150,000 people were working on what came to be known as 'The Manhattan Project'. All available atomic experts were pulled into the project and simply designated as 'scientific personnel who were obliged to submit to the strict rules of military secrecy'.

A professional soldier, General Groves, who had never experienced anything more warlike than a desk, was put in charge of the management of the entire project. He set about searching for a suitable American scientist to direct the work and to enlist the best minds amongst the nuclear physicists who had joined the exodus from Europe. His choice was Robert J. Oppenheimer who was by this time the professor of nuclear physics at the University of Berkeley in California.

Unlike the men he had studied under in Germany, who had made great discoveries as well as being teachers of distinction, Oppenheimer had not even by his fortieth year brought any epoch-making new ideas to light. Although his achievements might be considered exceptional by the academic world, he himself did not believe he had done enough and felt a sense of failure. It was at this point he was suddenly offered the opportunity to accomplish something of a very different nature – to take charge of the construction of the mightiest and most lethal weapon of all time.

The man, whose great charisma was once described as 'intellectual sex appeal', now used all his charm, shrewdness and manipulative powers to choose his immediate team, some of whom needed a great deal of persuasion to join him. It was his decision also to bring together in one particular spot all the vital aspects of the project, at that time spread across the USA, England and Canada. In this way the whole collective work would be under his own, single direction. But where could he find a site for the new laboratories which would secretly cradle the still unborn atom bomb? Various locations were suggested by others but Robert Oppenheimer was attracted to the remote spot at Los Alamos in New Mexico where he had once attended as a boy a rustic boarding school. In his former days he had facetiously told his friends, 'My two great loves are Physics and New Mexico. It's a pity they can't be combined.' Now at one stroke he combined them.

On a plateau of the foothills of the Jemez mountains, Los Alamos, surrounded by desert, was as remote as the Academy of Jundi-Shapur. It was also sited on a 'kiva' a holy place sacred to the local Indians. The utter isolation of the site had great appeal to General Groves to whom the secrecy of the project was of prime importance. On this site known to the Indians as *Oscuro*, or the place of darkness, there now gathered the nuclear physicists who had been expelled from their own countries. The one thing they shared was a disbelief in any other reality than the substratum of matter as explained by the theories of pure physics. The only form of worship they knew was the devotion to that materialism out of which the very building blocks of the universe would one day be explained. The very consequences of what they were doing were in their minds justified for the advancement of science. And such an attitude was also justified to the youth they had known as

143

'Oppie' because it was a pathway to the very pinnacle of scientific achievement and to the advancement of his own career.

As it turned out, the fear of Adolf Hitler developing the atomic bomb, which in the first place had engendered the frantic activity of the Manhattan Project, was completely unfounded. The leading atomic physicists in Germany had succeeded in doing their utmost to delay the making of the ultimate weapon and even at the end of the war in Europe their preparations were at least two years behind the American project. Hahn, who had been concerned in the first discovery of the fragmentation of the nucleus by the newly discovered neutrons, had said to his German colleagues: 'I only hope you will never construct a uranium bomb. If Hitler ever gets a weapon like that I'll commit suicide.' Heisenberg, the genius who discovered 'The Theory of Indeterminancy', made sure that this never came about, calling all attempts to apply nuclear physics to destructive purposes 'Service of the Devil'.

After the capitulation of the Third Reich when the Americans became the new claimants to the Spear of Destiny, the pace of work in the vast complex which had mushroomed in Los Alamos now increased considerably. The new justification for continuing the project was the belief that the atom bomb might bring the war with Japan to an immediate end. Throughout June and July 1945 there was a formidable heatwave and it seemed that the weather itself had conspired to frustrate the closed community who were building the bomb. A hot wind blew from the desert over the settlement and time and again the sky darkened and summer lightning flickered in the distance over the Sangre de Cristo mountains. The moment arrived to transport the components of the interior explosive mechanism of the experimental bomb to the *Jornado del Muerto* (tract of death) near the vacated village of Oscuro (the place of darkness). At this late moment on the threshold of a new era, many of the physicists and engineers involved began for the first time to have doubts about their moral involvement in a task which they could now visualize might have the most terrible consequences.

Amongst the leading physicists themselves a tremendous excitement was growing. They were reaching the moment of transition from the calculations and formulae of pure physics to the first successful outward manifestation of the truths they had found.

'Don't bother me with your conscientious scruples!' said Enrico Fermi to his hesitant colleagues. 'After all, the thing's superb physics.'

At Point Zero in the formidable isolation of the desert, the engineers had constructed a framework of iron scaffolding on which the atom bomb was to be set at the very last possible moment so as to avoid the danger of the thunderstorms which had continued intermittently throughout the final month of preparation. A conventional bomb of the same size had been fixed on the scaffolding some days earlier to test the conditions. In a sudden, mighty thunderstorm it had been struck by lightning and exploded with a loud bang. It was as though the Angel of the Lord, who once appeared in thunder and lightning on Golgotha, was giving the demonically inspired community of scientists a reminder of the words of Christ on the Cross: 'They know not what they do.'

'Human calculation indicates that the experiment must succeed,' Hans Bethe, head of the theoretical division, told the assembled scientists before they boarded buses *en route* to the vicinity of the test site. 'But will nature act in conformity with our calculations?'

At five thirty in the morning of 16 July the first atomic bomb was detonated. Everybody was transfixed with fear at the power of the explosion. Some felt that the bright ball of flame growing larger and larger would never stop until it had enveloped all heaven and earth. A passage from the *Bhagavad Gita*, the sacred epic of the Hindus, arose in the mind of Robert Oppenheimer as he watched in terrified fascination the monstrous physiognomy of this weapon from hell which broke forth with an awesome roar, reminding everyone present of doomsday, and making them feel it was a blasphemy to tamper with the forces of nature heretofore the sole preserve of the Almighty:

> If the radiance of a thousand suns
> Were to burst into the sky.
> That would be like
> The splendour of the Mighty One.

As a sinister and gigantic cloud arose in the distance above Point Zero, Oppenheimer was reminded of another line from the *Gita*:

> I am become Death, the shatterer of worlds.

Robert Oppenheimer, the prime architect of the bomb was wrong in identifying the effects of the explosion with Krishna, the Sun Logos, on his path of descent to earth to become Christ. Rather he beheld the terrible face of the Sun Demon, Azura, the third and mightiest of the trinity of evil whose avowed intent is to mutate the human form and destroy the planet earth.

Leo Szilard, the man responsible for alerting the American Government to the importance of manufacturing the atom bomb, now headed a large group of scientists at Oak Ridge in writing a petition to the Government urging that the new weapon should not be used against Japan without prior demonstration and opportunity to surrender. The petition, with a very large number of signatures from the participants in the Manhattan Project, also demanded an immediate study of the possibility of securing international control of the new weapon. General Groves decided that it was impossible to forbid his scientists to sign the document but he found a cunning method of stopping its further circulation. He immediately declared Szilard's petition a secret document. The law at that time stated that secret papers could only be taken from one place to another under military guard. 'Unfortunately,' said the General, 'we cannot spare any troops at the moment for the protection of this document. Until we can do so it must be kept locked up.'

General Groves's manipulative action in preventing the circulation of the petition had an unexpected result. Leo Szilard, who had so persistently lobbied President Roosevelt to make the bomb before Hitler had the opportunity, now employed the same dogged determination in his efforts to persuade President Truman not to use it on the Japanese now that Germany had been defeated. The scientist sought, and gained, an audience with Truman's most trusted adviser, Senator James Byrnes, at his home in Carolina. Szilard told Byrnes that he felt profoundly uneasy at the prospect of using the bomb on Japan.

Byrnes's reply was simple: 'Of course we will use the bomb on Japan. What worries me most is Russia's spreading influence in Eastern Europe. It will be impossible to persuade the Russians to remove troops from Poland without using the bomb.'

Szilard's answer was prophetic: 'If we use the bomb on Japan, we will start an arms race between Russia and the United States, and who knows where that may lead.'

Byrnes was unmoved by the scientist's pleas. Appointed by Truman to the influential 'Interim Committee', Byrnes persuaded them to advise the president that 'The view of this committee is that we should use the bomb on Japan as soon as possible.'

Few events in the annals of human civilization could truly be held to have 'changed the course of the history of the world for all time'. The dropping of the first atomic bombs as an act of war was clearly one of them. When we study the events leading to the decision to use the atomic bomb and the conflicting attitudes of the personalities involved in reaching that terrible decision, we see once more the truly demonic aspect of the twofold face of evil and sense the malignant influence of Behemoth on the process that would lead the entire world on a course towards self-destruction.

The death of President Franklin Delano Roosevelt and the subsequent inauguration of his successor, Harry S. Truman – a man with absolutely no experience whatsoever of foreign policy – as not only the President of the United States but also the supreme political leader of the Allies, was an opportunity Behemoth seized with alacrity. On 25 May 1945, within days of taking office, the inexperienced Truman expressed fears about the increasing confrontation between the western powers and their Russian allies. His Secretary of State for War, Henry Stimson, informed him about the 'Manhattan Project' and the proposed testing of the first atomic bomb. Stimson outlined his own fears arising from the problem of sharing the knowledge of how to manufacture this new bomb with their Russian allies. He stated insistently that this dilemma has become 'the primary question of our foreign relations'. He suggested that a 'quid pro quo' might be obtainable from the Russians, namely over the settlement of the political future of Poland. On hearing this, Truman decided not to discuss the question of Poland's future with Stalin until after the test had taken place and the bomb was seen to work.

It is clear from all the relevant documentation that from this moment the new President used every tactic possible to delay a meeting of 'The Big Three' until after the test date –

despite sustained and repeated pressure from Churchill to meet Stalin as soon as possible.

The closest and most influential advisor to the inexperienced Truman from the time of his unexpected accession to the presidency until the end of the war, was not Henry Stimson his Secretary of State for War, but Senator James Byrnes from South Carolina who was not even a member of the Government – yet Byrnes's role in the coming events was to be decisive.

Recently discovered documents give a new perspective to the political events that led to the awesome decision to drop the first atomic bombs on Japan. Dr Gar Alperovitz, author of *Atomic Diplomacy*, stated that historians who have studied these papers carefully, comparing and contrasting them with the official announcements made at the end of the war, have found disturbing discrepancies between the advice given to the President and his public pronouncements, pronouncements which clearly stated that the fateful decision to drop the bomb was made solely to force Japan to surrender and therefore save hundreds of thousands of American lives. Yet even on the very day of victory there were already many conflicting views expressed concerning the necessity of employing this appalling device against innocent civilians. These views contrasted sharply with the decision by this non-elected President, and tended to show the complete abandonment of conscience that led to the unnecessary use in war of such a fearsome weapon.

The 'Surrender Edition' of the *New York Times* on 15 August 1945 shows that even at that time there was considerable dispute regarding the necessity of dropping the bomb. The headline told of Japan's surrender, and of the role apparently played by the destruction of Hiroshima and Nagasaki. Other reports in the same paper told a different story. General Chenault is quoted as saying that the entry of Russia into the Japanese war was the decisive factor in

Japan's surrender, and would still have been even if the bomb had not been dropped. The Air Force General Curtis E. le May was reported as saying:

> The atomic bombs had nothing to do with the end of the war, even if they had not been dropped the war would have been over in two weeks without Russia's entry into that conflict.

With such opinions being quoted by senior military men, how did such a terrifying decision come to be made?

Other moves had been made to bring an end to the war. Truman knew from the Russians that Japan was putting out peace feelers, and had appointed Prince Konoye as plenipotentiary to negotiate with the Russians to persuade them to act as brokers in the peace process. Confirmation came from several sources. America had cracked the Japanese codes early in the war, and knew this from intelligence intercepts. 'Wild' Bill Donovan, head of the OSS (the precursor to the CIA), advised Truman that, in negotiating surrender, one of the few provisions Japan would insist upon was the retention of the Emperor. Allen Dulles told the President 'Japan does want to surrender.'

The Assistant Secretary of State, Joseph Groome, produced a draft statement to the Joint Chiefs of Staff in which he wrote: 'I think that we should consider any step which will persuade the Japanese to surrender now. If we can give indications that they may retain the Emperor, they will "save face" and surrender.' This attitude was reinforced by the Chief of the Imperial General Staff, Field Marshal Sir Alan Brooke, and given further strength by the comments of Churchill himself. General George Marshall put forward the view that the prospect of Russian participation in the war with Japan might be the decisive factor in persuading Japan to surrender. Groome's approach led him inevitably to Henry Stimson, who used delaying tactics, mentioning obliquely that there were 'military means to end the war that I am not at liberty to discuss'.

The vital role played by Byrnes and the real motivation of Truman himself did not become clear until the discovery of the 'misplaced' diaries of Harry Truman in the late seventies. These diaries, which had been kept secret from even the official archivist, clearly show that Byrnes regarded the Bomb as 'the gun behind the door'. He thought it 'a weapon powerful enough to destroy the entire world', and one which could help the United States dominate Russia after the war. Both Byrnes and Truman believed that America could keep her lead in the atomic field for ten years or more, little knowing that many of her atomic secrets were already in the hands of the Russians. Stalin's comments on the prospect of Japan's surrender were recorded at the Potsdam conference. Having told Truman of Japan's latest peace initiative, he said, 'This deserves a positive response – and that response must be no.' Thus the stage was set for the final decision.

The Supreme Allied Commander, General Dwight Eisenhower, was informed of the decision on 20 July. His response was simple: 'This decision is wrong – completely wrong. Japan is already defeated, why should we shock world opinion? This action is no longer necessary to save American lives.' His view was consigned to the dustbin of modern political history along with that of Szilard, Alan Brooke and Joseph Groome. For reasons that had no connection at all with the war with Japan, the decision had already been taken.

The first countdown to the demise of world peace for the next fifty years, began at Alamogordo, New Mexico on 16 July 1945, and the Cold War itself began with the blinding eruption of the first atomic fireball over the civilian city of Hiroshima on 6 August. Japan offered to surrender on

10 August, one day after Nagasaki had been needlessly destroyed.

Eisenhower unknowingly repeated the very point made by Leo Szilard, when he stated that:

'Before it was possible to keep peace with the Russians, now, I don't know. Everyone feels uneasy again.'

He was not the only American military leader to publicly express doubts about the morality of what had been done. The American Chief of Staff, Admiral Leahy, said:

'The use of that barbarous weapon was of no assistance in ending the war. I would not wish to make war in this way; I was not trained to make war against innocent women and children. By being the first to use this bomb, America has adopted an ethical standard common to the barbarians of the "Dark Ages".'

One of the few American Generals who publicly supported the decision to use the bomb was not surprisingly the officer commanding the 'Manhattan Project', General Groves. A General who had never heard a shot fired in anger throughout his long career.

Behemoth's influence upon the cumulative actions of patriotic men of narrow and blinkered vision, men who chose to ignore the opinions of the Generals whose courage and skill had led the Allied armies to the brink of victory, resulted in the commencement of an arms race which was to dominate world politics for nearly fifty years.

Thus the sum of a thousand individual acts of an intensely conscientious character led eventually to an act of collective abandonment of conscience, horrifying in its magnitude
Brighter than a Thousand Suns, p. 191: Robert Jungk

Two atomic bombs were dropped on the island of Japan; the targets were the innocent civilian cities of Hiroshima, causing 138,890 casualties, and Nagasaki, causing 48,857 more. The eventual total of all those killed or damaged by these two bombs is still not known.

'We did the Devil's work,' said Robert Oppenheimer, 'but we are now going back to our real jobs.' The sorcerer's apprentice had unleashed powers which he could no longer control.

As the scientists of the Los Alamos laboratories dispersed to the universities that were now eager to employ them, the radioactive desolation of Hiroshima and Nagasaki gave mute witness to the fact that the apocalyptic age had now begun under the shadow of the Pale Horse.

SECTION 4

LIFE IN THE SHADOW OF THE PALE HORSE

The Outpouring of the Vials of Wrath

Now, at the end of the twentieth century in the shadow of the Pale Horse, it has become apparent that the strange and frightening mythological symbolism of the Revelation of St John is indeed not simply a prophecy couched in arcane and obscure terminology, but validated commentary that can be verified with complete objectivity by a scientific study of recent and contemporary events.

If we collate all the available information spewed forth in such a torrent by the media, cross index the various catastrophic events in all parts of the globe, and add to this scientific data about the world ecology, we can only reach an astonishing conclusion.

The mythological symbolism of the Revelation has become a magic mirror in which the dreaded face of the Apocalypse peers out from the reflection of recent, contemporary and coming events. In some instances the message in the archaic phraseology is confirmed by the findings and predictions of modern science.

155

CHAPTER TWELVE

THERE SHALL BE WARS AND RUMOURS OF WARS, BUT THE END IS NOT YET NIGH

> When you hear of wars and rumours of wars, do not be alarmed. Such things must happen, but the end is still to come. Nation will rise against nation, and kingdom against kingdom. ... These are the beginning of birth pains.
> The Gospel of St Mark (New International Version), 13: verses 7, 8

Dulce et decorum est, pro patria mori.

The doors of the vault in the *Oberen Schmied Gasse* in Nuremberg were reopened on 4 January 1946 and the Spear of Destiny was returned to Austria on the orders of General Dwight Eisenhower, the Commander of the Allied Armies in Europe. The Spear along with other imperial treasures was loaded aboard a Dakota at Fürth Airport and flown directly to Vienna. Two days later – 6 January – General Mark Clark handed over the *Reichskleinodien* and the *Reichsheiligtümer* to the *Bürgermeister* of Vienna. It was a short informal ceremony with no official speeches. It appears that nobody was conscious of the real significance of this talisman of world destiny.

The Americans, while claimants to the Spear, had inaugurated the atomic age and had been the prime movers in founding the United Nations. As a temporary expedient the slightly embarrassed *Bürgermeister* deposited the Spear along with the rest of the defunct Habsburg regalia in the vault of the Austrian Postal Savings Bank. It appears that the Spear rested unclaimed and unnoticed until it was returned to the same spot in the Treasure House where Adolf Hitler first beheld it in 1909. Now for the first time it had significance for any individual who saw in it the key to unveiling personal destiny. But its world significance at this time remained hidden to all but the initiated. For over the state of Austria under four-power occupation, the two emerging apocalyptic beasts, represented by America and the USSR, growled alarmingly at each other in the opening rounds of 'The Cold War' in which the world trembled on the brink of atomic annihilation.

The helpless impotence of all peoples who now faced the atomic peril was exacerbated by the disclosure in 1947 by Molotov that the atomic bomb held no secrets from the Russians. This was confirmed by radioactive evidence of a Russian nuclear explosion which was detected by the West during 1949. The development of an 'improved' nuclear weapon, the thermo-nuclear or hydrogen bomb, in 1952 hastened mankind's head-long race to destruction, Russia being only months behind America in developing this more 'sophisticated' and destructive device. Both sides were soon able to devise rocket systems to deliver the bombs, using the expertise of German engineers recruited from the ranks of Hitler's scientists. The balance of terror, known as 'Mutually Assured Destruction', had begun.

The linking of the rocket and the atom bomb created the weapon which still dominates the military and political scene today. In this connection, it is worth looking more closely at the effects of rockets and atomic energy, for they reveal a curious and instructive polarity of what we have already described as the twofold face of evil.

When an atomic bomb explodes, the awesome nuclear fireball it produces is transfigured with a terrible glory, revealing briefly the Luciferic light which inspired this demonic device. The atomic bomb is thus seen to be,

157

outwardly at least, the inspiration of Lucifer.

Its use and its consequences reveal the other face of evil, for both are Ahrimanic in nature. The byproducts of the ultimate destructive power devised by man, radioactive debris, have an ageing effect on the earth. Fall-out is the physical equivalent of the psychological effect that the fear of these weapons induces. This fear has engendered new military strategies such as 'The Balance of Terror' or 'Graduated Deterrence', founded upon a mathematical, mechanical, cold, inhuman logic. The concept of 'Defending Freedom and Democracy' is held to justify the appalling means – Mutually Assured Destruction.

In the outward aspect of the large rockets we again discern the lateral inversion of the two-fold face of evil. They seem a wholly Ahrimanic inspiration, combining unimaginable, yet controlled power in their engines, with a cold, calculating, electronic guidance system. The engine resembles a beautifully engineered digestive system that imbibes fuel and excretes great gouts of flame, which then impel the rocket violently spacewards. The mechanical eyes, radar and navigational systems, combine to target the machine precisely – automatically correcting any errors – on its predestined, demonic and destructive course half-way across the globe.

The terror that John Davy, formerly a science correspondent for the *Observer*, describes as the counterpart of the radioactive fall-out is not only preparing the way towards an overall world power as the only means of overcoming this fear, but has also legitimized a whole series of wars since 1945 whose appalling human cost exceeds the total casualty list of the Second World War many times over. Without the ever-present nightmare of a thermo-nuclear holocaust it is unthinkable that humanity would have allowed this whole chain of violence to have continued unchecked for four decades. The true obscenity of nuclear weapons lies in the legitimization of the acceptability of conflict using 'conventional' weapons, any war irrespective of its cause or motivation being deemed preferable to Armageddon.

Many of these conflicts were direct continuations of the Second World War itself, and in their initial stages proceeded almost unnoticed by the war-weary people of America and Western Europe. The continuing civil war in China between the red armies of Mao Tse-tung and the Nationalists led by Chiang Kai-shek, a man who was described by the Supreme Allied Commander in the Pacific, Lord Louis Mountbatten, as totally mad, did not reach its bloody conclusion until 1949. The casualties that resulted from this conflict alone reached a total of many millions, and with the war's end a period of tension and distrust began which had far-reaching effects on American foreign and military policy for nearly four decades. The parallel situation in Eastern Europe, where the Iron Curtain had descended separating the Communist states from their Democratic counterparts in the West, reinforced the seemingly inevitable growth and rapacity of world-wide Communism in its march towards world domination. From this point on, politicians began to speak publicly about the Communist third of the world, and all their public and private actions and policies reflected their fear of further growth of Communist power and influence.

Reaction took many forms, not only the inevitable violent reaction of the old imperial nations such as Britain, France and Holland against their various subject States struggling for independence, but also the intervention of the USA in the affairs of any State that was deemed to be vulnerable to Communist influence or takeover. American influence was exerted in many ways, by alliances such as NATO and SEATO, by economic influence and by more or less direct political interference in the internal affairs of other States in every continent.

159

Russia in its turn took a similar course, forming an alliance with its subject States in Eastern Europe as a result of the Warsaw Pact. This bastion of Communist equality of opportunity also became an effective, if sometimes none too subtle, expert in the art of destabilization, infiltration and political blackmail in order to bend other States to its will. America was not the only superpower to create puppet governments who then invited their patrons and creators to 'defend' them. Russia played this particular 'diplomatic' game with the consummate skill of a great chess-playing nation. Once again the lateral inversion of the mirror image of the two faces of evil became apparent in the reactions of both the opposing superpowers.

The Soviet Union, with its centralized authority and its emphasis on the state rather than the individual, clearly arises from an Ahrimanic influence. Yet this conception, with its cold, calculating machinery of repression, has been forced upon a people whose innate impulses are religious – a religiosity which Lucifer has lead astray.

In the USA the reverse situation is reflected. The values of this capitalist state, 'Freedom', 'Democracy' and 'Private Enterprise', are considered to be the ultimate virtues. Russia is feared and called 'The Evil Empire'. The USA is the home of mass production, where mass persuasion through advertising – propaganda raised to an art form – and mechanical efficiency, are deemed as concepts of major virtue. Thus Ahrimanic influences are clearly at work at the very heart of American society.

The world has been in a constant state of war since 1945, but public perception of this appalling fact has been masked by the language of 'doublespeak' so well described by George Orwell in his perceptive novel *1984*. Wars are no longer referred to as wars, but are spoken of in polite and more innocuous euphemisms such as 'emergencies', 'terrorist activities', rebellions against legitimate governments, uprisings, periods of 'political unrest' and spasmodic 'destabilization'. The language of true communication has been devalued and replaced with the deliberate purveying, not of propaganda, but of 'disinformation' which has lulled entire nations into accepting the unacceptable as a natural consequence of political existence. Thus mankind in both East and West have been denied the vision of the true facts through which they could have perceived the real face of the Apocalypse in the mirror of contemporary events within the changing scenes of the times.

Deliberate disinformation, destruction of countries and economies, defoliation of forests and the ever-lengthening casualty lists were not the only evil consequence of the many wars which have taken place in our lifetime. Basic human values are the real casualty of this period. This process has been accelerated and reinforced by western man's constant exposure to vivid, visual images of war as it takes place, brought into his home on a daily basis by the wonders of modern technology – television and communication satellites. This constant stream of almost inescapable picture images dulls his senses irrevocably to the spiritual reality that lies behind death and destruction until, by repetition, war and all its consequences are seen as a normal part of life – and then not really perceived at all.

When the concentration camps, genocide and torture of the Third Reich were finally revealed in 1945, the peoples of the world were so horrified they swore that such crimes against humanity must never happen again. Sadly today such crimes are commonplace, accepted as an integral part of the normal currency of political confrontation in many countries, and pass unremarked elsewhere. This apparent acceptance is not based on the silence of assent, but on the impotence of fear and helplessness against the international political machine.

161

Concentration camps and forcible deportations are no longer the monopoly of the Nazis, but have been used by the British in Malaya and Kenya, the French in Indo-China and Algeria, for the 'political re-education' of dissidents in Communist countries in Asia. They probably reached their most developed and terrifying form in the 'Gulags' of Soviet Russia, not only under Stalin, but also under the majority of his successors.

Torture has become commonplace throughout the world. It is not the sole preserve of the dictatorships of South America, who, incidentally, employed many Nazi experts in this art – including Klaus Barbie the 'Butcher of Lyon' – but this pernicious habit has spread into general and accepted use by many of the so-called civilized nations of Europe. Britain was convicted before the International Court at the Hague on charges of torture arising out of its activities in Northern Ireland. France's unenviable record in this respect in Algeria, Indo-China and in Metropolitan France itself during the OAS 'troubles' is well known. The most proficient 'experts' in this dubious field however are said to be the Chinese with their 'brainwashing' techniques and the record of the Soviet Union in its systematic use of torture during the great purge, and the misuse of psychiatric hospitals to 're-educate' dissidents, is a matter of world-wide concern and cricitism.

Atrocities and war crimes have multiplied since 1945. Sadly, many nations have learnt only too well from the examples that were set during the Second World War. With a few notable exceptions where the international conscience has been aroused, such as over the My Lai massacre in Vietnam, the incidence of torture in Chile, the plight of certain well-known dissidents in the USSR, most of these 'incidents' have passed almost unnoticed by the public at large.

Few people seem to be able to remember and retain

information for long enough to draw a full coherent picture of the continuing, escalating vortex of horror that represents the recent history of man's inhumanity to man. Under the constant barrage of a flood of apparently disconnected information, the human mind reels in confusion – disinformation has now reached the status of a fine art within which truth can be revealed in such a way that it cannot actually be perceived and understood. Brutality and terror, allied to indifference to the fate of others and the devaluing of the humanity of the 'enemy' as somehow subhuman, has justified and legitimized terror so that it seems innocuous compared to the appalling consequences of Mutually Assured Destruction. This acceptance of terror and brutality has enabled leaders of some nations to introduce and use previously banned forms of weapons without effective protest. The existence of thermo-nuclear arsenals and the threat they pose has legitimized the use of chemical weapons and the development of germ warfare. This is the true measure of the quality of the peace that is gained under the shadow of deterrence.

The use of terror as an effective political weapon on a smaller scale has been clearly demonstrated in nearly all the so-called wars of liberation since 1945: Malaya – where it was used by both sides – Vietnam, Cyprus, Palestine and its successor state Israel, Algeria, Kenya, Afghanistan, Lebanon, Aden, Abyssinia and throughout Europe by groups as diverse as the IRA, the Baader-Meinhof gang, the Angry Brigade, various Palestinian organizations and, in Lebanon, by the Hezbollah. In a more subtle form, terror based on social, economic and political sanctions against the individual reached its peak in America during the McCarthy era. None of this could have happened unless the peoples of the world were paralysed by fear into accepting without question a total reversal of the values they had so universally affirmed in 1945. This degeneration in accepted values and behaviour reaches into the international political arena in the activities of both the diplomatic and the security services where it is universally believed that 'the end justifies the means'.

Prior to the Second World War, international espionage was almost at the adventure-story level of a few enthusiastic amateurs whose bumbling incompetence was only exceeded by their enthusiasm.

The war changed all that as the high price paid in human lives for this amateurish approach became unacceptable. Each of the belligerent nations developed espionage systems which rapidly acquired the necessary skills in subterfuge, deception and infiltration to acquire and process the information on which the fate of nations and the world depended. In the atmosphere of mutual distrust and hostility of the Cold War this tendency was reinforced and extended, not only by the two opposing superpowers but also by all the nations who felt that their continued existence was threatened by internal or external forces. The very scientific nature of the information sought imposed as a basic requirement a much higher degree of professional and intellectual competence than was previously needed. New technology changed both the methods and the evaluation of espionage so that the services became specialized and departmentalized.

Listening devices, satellite surveillance systems and the activities of the British GCHQ at Cheltenham and elsewhere have, with their counterparts in other countries, produced a bewildering and massive flood of information. This vast degree of input, analysed by computers in Britain and in Langley, Virginia – to say nothing of Russian activities – needs a precise form of analysis and targeting to become meaningful. Every possible means to acquire precisely targeted information is used or is under exploration by the intelligence services of all the major nations. The

164

morality, means and objectives of the espionage or intelligence services is to pursue the aims of the Cold War with a judicious admixture of nationalistic chauvinism. All the hypocrisy, disinformation and doublespeak that have so aided the general acceptance of the decline of international standards of behaviour have pervaded the clandestine arm of international politics as they have the *ouvert* area. All wars, subversive activities and acts of espionage since 1945 have been justified in the name of freedom, democracy or the rights of man and have resulted in the enslavement of peoples to ideologies of left or right, the denial of democracy and the continuous and progressive erosion of civil rights.

Doublespeak, mass communication and the highly professional level of disinformation have continued to mask the apocalyptic reality facing mankind under the shadow of the Pale Horse. Deluded by his apparent material comfort and bemused by the quantity and variety of the constantly changing imagery of mass communication, mankind's separation from spiritual reality is almost total. Even modern technology, by mimicking certain of the ancient initiation techniques, leads mankind deeper into materialism and further from the spiritual realities that lie behind the terrestrial world.

Humanity as a whole is standing at the threshold of the spiritual world. It is not difficult to recognize this situation. At the same time most people are not aware that almost every field of human endeavour and exploration reaches across and beyond the threshold itself. For example, space exploration quite clearly attempts to cross the threshold to enter that universe out of which the human soul is born and to which it will ultimately return on death. For this reason it is striking that in the science and technology of the space programmes we see a kind of caricature of the ancient trials of initiation which orientated the novice to the startling anatomy of inner space, preparing him for the new dimensions of

165

experience he was about to encounter. Such trials were universal in all initiation techniques and were called the Air, Water and Fire Trials.

The political will and the technological and scientific skill that have come together to develop the space programme, are almost certainly inspired by a Luciferic impulse – one that reflects and plays on man's desire to reach back to his early spiritual origins. It is nothing less than an attempt to return to, and communicate with, 'the Heavens'.

Crammed into their capsules, like twins or triplets in the womb, the space men undergo a form of rebirth – a modern day caricature of spiritual initiation. From countdown, through lift off, and throughout the flight and re-entry, physical conditions for the astronaut mimic the trials of the initiate. Subjected to forces in excess of five times the normal gravitational force in his attempt to break free from his own planet, the astronaut can truly be said to undergo 'Trial by Earth'. Floating weightlessly during flight in the womb-like capsule – like a foetus suspended in the amniotic fluid of its mother – he mimics 'Trial by Water'. Re-entry, protected by the 'heat shield' from all the heat engendered by the friction of the earth's atmosphere against the space capsule, he completes the cycle of apparent initiation with a terrifyingly real 'Trial by Fire'.

It is ironic that this caricature of true initiation has such a perverse effect on mankind as a whole. The physical fact of man's landing on the moon is used to demonstrate his mastery of the physical world and ignores spiritual reality altogether. The stated motive for space exploration, to extend man's understanding of the universe, not only distorts this apparent contradiction between the physical world and the spiritual but also belies its true aim – to gain mastery of space for offensive and warlike reasons. The space race is in fact, just another aspect of the cold-war confrontation that has helped to perpetuate and extend the areas of conflict and the threat of destruction over the entire planet.

The perceived fruits of space exploration for the majority of the population of the developed world can be summed up in two words, Teflon and computers! The only discernible benefits for the average westerner are therefore non-stick saucepans and word-processors! For the armaments manufacturers however they have presented a cornucopia of ever-increasing orders and profits.

The main cargo of the many space rockets has been satellites, some indeed used for apparently peaceful purposes such as navigation and weather forecasting but mainly intended for increased military surveillance and now, with the 'Star Wars' concept, for actual warfare itself. Wars have already taken place in which military intelligence gathered by satellites has played a vital part. The long-drawn-out agony of Vietnam, the Afghanistan invasion, the Falklands campaign and the present conflicts in Central America have all been monitored and influenced by this new technology.

While the Spear of Destiny rests undisturbed in the neutral State of Austria, mankind has entered fully into the apocalyptic age of the Pale Horse whose rider is Death and whose following are the Hosts of Hell. The two-fold face of evil has drawn together the threads of fear induced by the atomic age, the paranoia of the intelligence services, the depersonalization of modern technological 'defence' systems and superpower rivalry and have woven them not into a strand or rope, but into a 'Gordian Knot' of ever-present terror. This Gordian Knot cannot be unravelled but only cut by one of two means – world destruction or world dictatorship.

CHAPTER THIRTEEN

SCENARIO FOR WORLD DISASTER

Then the seven angels who had the seven trumpets prepared to sound them.

The first angel sounded his trumpet, and there came hail and fire mixed with blood, and it was hurled down upon the earth. A third of the earth was burned up, a third of the trees were burned up, and all the green grass was burned up.

The second angel sounded his trumpet, and something like a huge mountain, all ablaze, was thrown into the sea. A third of the sea turned into blood, a third of the living creatures in the sea died, and a third of the ships were destroyed.

The third angel sounded his trumpet, and a great star, blazing like a torch, fell from the sky on a third of the rivers and on the springs of water — the name of the star is Wormwood. A third of the waters turned bitter, and many people died from the waters that had become bitter.

The fourth angel sounded his trumpet, and a third of the sun was struck, a third of the moon, and a third of the stars, so that a third of them turned dark. A third of the day was without light, and also a third of the night.

As I watched, I heard an eagle that was flying in mid-air call out in a loud voice: 'Woe! Woe! Woe to the inhabitants of the earth, because of the trumpet blasts about to be sounded by the other three angels!'

Revelation (New International Version): 8, verses 6–13

The whole concept of world disaster as described in such biblical terms by St John in the Revelation at first glance appears to bear no apparent relationship to modern man surrounded by his material comforts in the so-called developed western world. Man today sees himself not as a part of a material and spiritual reality living in harmony with the planet of which he is such an integral part, but rather as an involuntary, if somewhat comfortable, passenger on 'Spaceship Earth' hurtling towards a destination he did not seek and cannot understand. His only choice seems to be as to how comfortable he can make his journey. If he has doubts and fears, and he assuredly does, they lie in the realm of the probability of thermo-nuclear war and he fails to perceive the potential for world disaster based on natural causes, or on any human cause other than nuclear holocaust.

What perception does modern 'scientific man' have of his present situation, and on what factual basis is that conception based? In answering this question, there at first appear to be only two totally contradictory schools of thought, the materialist scientific school and the fundamentalist religious approach. Each seems to be completely inimical to the other, and both, we submit, while containing some truth, are incomplete and therefore in error.

We have shown in our earlier chapters the descent of human consciousness from universal thinking to individual human thinking and demonstrated how responsibility was gradually passed to man to take on the direction of his own future development. Modern biologists have also realized an aspect of this – that man has now reached a unique position on the earth in which he is no longer the passive subject of external forces but can take his future into his own hands and begin to mould his own environment. For instance Julian Huxley writes in his famous essay *The Evolutionary Process*:

The present situation represents a remarkable point in the development of our planet – the critical point in which the evolutionary process now embodied in man, has for the first time become aware of itself, and has a dawning realisation of the possibilities of its future guidance or control. In other words, evolution is on the verge of becoming internalised, conscious, and self-directing.

Now we stand at the spiritual threshold and become aware of ourselves as beings of spirit, soul and body. And from this viewpoint we can no longer regard evolution as an accident, nor can we regard the physical state of the planet today as an accident, because they are both part of a great design. Unlikely as it might at first appear, the great catastrophes prophesied by St John are also regarded as highly probable from a purely objective, scientific point of view. When we test this probability from the historical and scientific aspects we will be in a position to perceive the spiritual perspective behind contemporary and coming events and discern the close relationship between scientifically observed facts and the prophecies of St John.

The record of natural disasters on a grand scale reaches back beyond written historical records into the realm of mythology and celestial history. The single event which is recorded in the mythology of many peoples and all great religions is the Flood, the Judaeo-Christian account of which is recorded in Genesis and which is linked in the traditions of the northern peoples with the myth of Atlantis. Tangible physical evidence is still extant of other great disasters which had a massive effect on the known world in an earlier stage of the evolution of consciousness of man. Perhaps the most widely known of these lies in the popular tourist site of ancient Pompeii, where today modern man can see direct evidence of the impact of natural phenomena on mankind who had ignored the vital life forces of the earth. Pompeii was not the only example of volcanic destruction which had a devastating effect on early Mediterranean civilizations, the destruction of the island now known as Santorini is merely one more example among many.

Floods, tidal waves and volcanic eruptions have continued to remind mankind of the awesome power of the natural world throughout recorded history. If we study the widespread effects of the eruption of Krakatoa in the Pacific Ocean during the last century we can begin to appreciate how far-reaching the immediate effects of such a catastrophe can be. The longer-term changes not only in the configuration of the landscape but also in the climatic effects which can occur as a result of this type of disaster were once more reinforced after the recent explosive eruption of Mount St Helens in the north west of the United States of America. Climatic change caused by the masking of the sun's rays by the immense and persistent clouds of volcanic debris, which circled the globe many times, gave a vivid if relatively small-scale foretaste of the possible 'nuclear winter' effect which scientists from all over the globe predict as the most likely outcome of full-scale nuclear war.

Volcanic eruptions are relatively rare in populated areas. More common, and widely feared, are earthquakes and earth movements which are endemic in many parts of the globe and have from time immemorial caused panic, destruction and widespread devastation. When taken in conjunction with flood and fire which often accompany them, whole civilizations have been destroyed or have had to modify their entire pattern of living in order to accommodate to the probability of their constant recurrence. The traditional architecture of Japan is largely derived from just such an accommodation with the ever-present threat of earthquake, while Norse mythology and the entire way of life of the Icelandic people reflects quite vividly man's ability to cope with the continuance of similar threats from volcanic activity.

The scientific study of earth movements, earthquakes

171

and seismology has established a growing body of evidence that mankind in general seems to ignore in its entirety. The pattern of geological faults and points of juncture of the tectonic plates are by now well known to the seismologists, and prolonged study of earth tremors and movements is providing sufficient evidence to be able to predict that minor tremors of certain patterns of intensity, often give advance warning of larger earthquakes in the vicinity.

One of the most intensely studied geographical areas subject to earthquakes is the territory surrounding the line of the San Andreas Fault which runs down the densely populated western seaboard of the United States of America. Density of population in areas subject to larger earthquakes is therefore not restricted to the older parts of civilization but, despite present scientific knowledge, occurs in the newer areas also. This has been proved with tragic intensity in the earthquakes which have taken place in relatively old cities, such as Managua in Central America, Tashkent in the Soviet Union as well as in the more modern city of Leninakan in Soviet Armenia.

The probability of massive earth movements occurring again in the vicinity of California is well known and celebrated in a variety of works of fiction both written and cinematic. The underlying truth is such that the title Alistair Maclean chose for one of his books, *Goodbye California*, could well prove to be prophetic. A fascinating melange of scientific fact, seismological theory and psychic perception provided the basis of *The Earthquake Generation*, a book which achieved a wide circulation in the USA and catered to the inherent fears of many of its readers. One theory proposed in that work is that massive earthquakes could remove California, parts of New Mexico and much of the West Coast from the present seaboard of the United States. This may disclose more about the levels of fear that exist than it does about the probable reality, but we must not

172

blind ourselves to the fact that much of California is quite definitely at risk.

A fascinating study also originating from California was published in *The New Scientist* in England in July 1988. This series of observations and conclusions by Jim Shirley, a scientist based in California, did not directly touch on the subject of seismology, but instead put forward some disturbing thoughts about sunspot activity. Accurate records of sunspot activity date from the 1840s; other records do exist, but not with the same level of reliability. The sunspot cycle undergoes periodic cyclical changes, and Shirley notes that the sun is now beginning an unusual retrograde loop in its orbit, an event that has been extremely rare since any form of records began. It is claimed that this phenomenon has only occurred twice before in the last thirteen hundred years. On both previous occasions, during the periods 1623–33 and 1810–12, intense bursts of volcanic activity 'shook the earth' and the climate cooled sharply. Shirley estimates the likelihood of these occurrences happening simultaneously with the solar orbit of this type accidentally, has a probability of about 4 per cent. He therefore predicts that a similar period of volcanic activity and climatic change is highly probable on this occasion.

Important as these aspects of disaster may be they do not at present pose the greatest threat to mankind today. Nuclear war in all its horror and potential for destruction is placed fairly low down on the scale of events that threaten the continued existence of our civilization. What then is the most likely cause of world disaster on anything like the scale envisaged by St John in the vivid imagery he uses in the Revelation? The greatest threat of all comes from man's own lifestyle, which in many aspects tends to destroy the complex relationships that underpin the continuing inter-dependence of the various eco-systems that constitute the physical reality we call the natural world. Added to this damaging ignorance of the physical reality of nature's fragile relationship is a blank incomprehension of the spiritual reality that lies behind it. There is a growing body of evidence that pollution of the environment in its many forms has already created the irreversible process that leads inevitably to world disaster.

What is pollution? Pollution can be defined as any interference by man with the natural world that adversely affects not merely man himself, but the ecology as a whole. The growing awareness of the dangers of pollution affects each individual in different ways. Industrial pollution arising from and restricted to local situations has been known for centuries. In many areas generations have lived close to the physical evidence of this form of pollution, slag heaps in mining communities and the polluted and despoiled rivers that drain major industrial sites being perhaps the most obvious. The far distant effects that can arise from man's attempts to increase his living standards and efficiency are in many cases much more difficult to discern until they have become a serious and sometimes irreversible threat — usually to communities far from the site that caused them.

The pressure to increase food production, allied to new knowledge of pesticides and fertilizers, has brought about one of the more serious and widespread types of environmental damage to affect the European continent. The run-off from arable land of excess fertilizers into the rivers and lakes that drain our farmlands has disturbed the ecosystems that maintain the purity of our rivers and destroyed the habitats of the wildlife that lives in and around them. When allowed to degenerate along this path, well-aerated waterways become completely de-oxygenated, anaerobic, almost lifeless sewers. Instead of providing refreshing means of sustenance for the fish and fowl that play such an important part in the ecology of the countryside, the rivers become running sewer-like repositories of algae and bacteria that breed in the anaerobic and de-oxygenated environment that has been created. This process can only be reversed with great difficulty and over long periods of time. The process is called eutrofication and affects many rivers in the north of England, rivers, lakes and part of the fiords of Norway and Sweden, the lakes of Switzerland, the Rhine, and the Great Lakes in the USA. Many a lake-side dwelling on the shores of Lake Michigan is now virtually unsaleable due to the unpleasant environmental change that has taken place.

This process is not restricted to the European and North American Continents, but tends to happen wherever man has used massive fertilization programmes to increase food production. In Europe the situation has been further complicated by an additional source of pollution – a particularly long-range one – the problem of acid rain. Acid rain falls far from the sites that cause it. The addition of large quantities of both carbon and sulphur dioxides from the burning of fossil fuels acidifies the rain-bearing clouds which carry the now acidified rain over long distances until it is precipitated many hundreds of miles away from the offending source. In this way the forests and plant life of Germany, Scandinavia and the Baltic States are being subjected to a constant barrage of acid rainfall which is destroying them at a truly appalling rate and, despite the protests of the affected nations, the main offender – Great Britain – does nothing at all to terminate the cause. It has long been known that a cleansing process can be used at source which is capable of ending this problem totally for a small capital cost, but British industry continues to do nothing with the active connivance of its Government, a Government which has recently deferred effective action by insisting on a pilot scheme involving a few power stations to prove what is already known and accepted by its European neighbours. Thus remedial action is deferred in Britain for at least five or ten years. The record of the British Government is at least reliable – they not only import other countries' dangerous waste products, chemical and radioactive, but they allow pollution of their own land and coastline too, with scant regard for the consequences.

The Irish Sea, from the southern tip of the Isle of Man to the North Wales coast, is nearing ecological death brought about by the pollution washed into it from the rivers draining England's industrial heartland, compounded by the use of the sea as a repository for shiploads of industrial waste, surplus wartime ammunition and last of all the deliberate discharge of nuclear by-products from the nuclear reprocessing plant at Sellafield. Britain is far from being the only offender in this regard. An ecological survey of many of the rivers and forests of Canada would reflect the problems that affect Northern Europe, while the east coast of the USA is hardly a showplace of ecological conservation. The west coast of the USA and the east coast of Britain are both centres of oil production, and the piecemeal destruction of the marine ecology that results from the frequent spillages, accidents and disasters is cumulatively damaging. Sadly the rivers and seas are not the only areas to be affected by radioactive pollution, which is perceived in the public mind as possibly the greatest threat.

Radioactive by-products of the nuclear power industry with their lethal side-effects and their unbelievably long half-life have become the bogeyman that haunts the dreams and nightmares of the entire population of the developed world. Not only is mankind technologically incapable of devising means safely to dispose of such waste, but the official pronouncements about safety are viewed with a mixture of cynicism and fear by the public at which they are directed; a cynicism that is compounded and exacerbated by Her Majesty's Government's actions designed to allay public fears about the safety of the Nuclear Fuel Reprocessing Plant. The action they take is very simple, and its timing predictable. Every time public concern reaches a high peak, the Government simply changes the name of the establishment. In this simple but effective way it is difficult for the average member of the public to know exactly what is happening where, particularly when the effects of bureaucratic secrecy are taken into account.

A growing body of evidence and experience is accumulating which indicates with increasing force the link between cancer and leukaemia incidence in the areas surrounding nuclear installations. Local 'small scale accidents' have adversely affected farmland, livestock and crops in the vicinity of nuclear power stations, and, despite official secrecy and reticence, are becoming widely known. Full-scale disasters are no longer a matter of statistical possibility or even probability, they have already happened. Three Mile Island, Windscale and the greatest of all to date that of Chernobyl prove that industrial accidents of world-threatening magnitude have occurred. The Chernobyl incident destroyed farmlands in the Ukraine over an immense area, spread through radioactive clouds of contamination over much of western Europe and is at present still discernible in the atmosphere over much of the globe as we write.

> The third angel sounded his trumpet, and a great star, blazing like a torch, fell from the sky on a third of the rivers and on the springs of water – the name of the star is Wormwood.
>
> The Revelation of St John (New International Version): 8, verses 10–11.

The English translation of the Russian name Chernobyl is Wormwood.

There is one aspect of pollution that overshadows all of

those we have previously mentioned, one which in the opinion of the scientific community not merely can bring about world-scale disaster but has already progressed a long way along that path. This arises from man's greed and rapacity on the one hand and his love for fast food and convenience products on the other – the greenhouse effect.

The first intimations of this reaction were seen as long ago as 1827 by the French mathematician Baron Joseph Fourier who noted that carbon dioxide warmed the atmosphere and could possibly affect climatic conditions. It was, however, the Swedish scientist Svante Arrhenius who actually coined the term 'the greenhouse effect' to describe the build-up of carbon dioxide and its climatic consequences.

Carbon dioxide in the upper atmosphere has the same effect as glass in a greenhouse, allowing the sun's rays through to warm the earth, but trapping much of the heat which would otherwise be dissipated back into space when reflected from the surface of the earth. The naturally occurring levels of carbon dioxide result from the interchange that takes place between the earth's production of the gas and its conversion back into oxygen by trees and other plant life. This would normally keep the earth's temperature at an average level of 15°C, ideal conditions for the maintenance of human life and its support systems as we know them.

The level of this important constituent of the atmosphere is increasing rapidly due to several man-made causes. Mankind has been burning fossil fuels at an ever-increasing rate for the last hundred years or so, and this high rate has increased during the later part of this century to a truly formidable figure. We emit 5.4 billion tonnes of carbon dioxide every year from this source alone, and this rate of release is increasing at a yearly rate in excess of 100 million tonnes per year. To this figure must be added the relatively new menace of chlorofluorocarbon gases used as propellants in aerosols, released from refrigeration units and also a by-product every time the new packaging for fast foods is used. This gas exacerbates the situation as each molecule of CFC gas released traps 10,000 times more heat than one molecule of carbon dioxide.

Chlorofluorocarbon gases have another potentially lethal effect on the ecology; they are destroying the ozone layer in the upper atmosphere, which is part of our defence system against the harmful effects of solar radiation. There is now a discernible 'hole' in the ozone layer in the Antarctic region that is getting perceptibly bigger. Joseph Farman of the British Antarctic Survey reported to the House of Commons Environment Committee that 'we have wiped out the heart of the Ozone layer. This implies that there is a sort of threshold ... and once you have got above that threshold, then things go. Our problem is that we do not know if there is a threshold for greenhouse gases above which "things will go".' The good news is that in many of the countries of the western world CFC gases are now banned from use in aerosols as a result of the agreement reached in Montreal, the so called 'Montreal Protocol'. The disturbing factor few take into consideration is the masking effect caused by the change in the sunspot activity and solar orbit. The cooling effects of that are masking the full impact of the greenhouse effect and the depletion of the ozone layer, according to the California scientist Jim Shirley.

There is yet another gas which exacerbates the greenhouse effect, and that gas is nitrous oxide, which occurs naturally as part of the life cycle of the biological activities in soil and water. Nitrous oxide is also used as a dental anaesthetic – being more commonly called 'laughing gas'. The scientists are now using black humour to make their point: 'If we are to die from the greenhouse effect, at least we'll all die laughing.'

The greenhouse effect is also made worse by the ruthless exploitation of the tropical rain forests. Cutting down trees on the massive scale that has taken place in recent years not only severely reduces the earth's natural capacity to transform carbon dioxide into oxygen, but also releases more carbon dioxide when the trees themselves are burnt. The subsequent use of the cleared ground for cattle ranching adds another damaging factor to the equation. The digestive process of cattle produces large quantities of methane, yet another greenhouse gas also produced as a by-product of nearly every form of organic degeneration. To all of this we must add the effect of nitrous oxide which is produced in large quantities wherever fertilizers are used. In these complex and ever-increasing ways the 'glass' in our terrestrial greenhouse becomes thicker every year.

Evidence to this effect is mounting and being collated at the headquarters of the United Nations Environmental Programme in Nairobi. A leading climatic expert attached to NASA, Dr James Hansen, recently told a United States Congressional Committee that in his opinion he was 99 per cent certain that the greenhouse effect was responsible for the present great drought affecting the grain areas of the American Midwest. He also told politicians that:

'We can state with 99% confidence that current temperatures represent a real warming trend rather than a chance fluctuation . . . It is time to stop waffling so much and say that the evidence is pretty strong that the Greenhouse Effect is here.'

These warnings were echoed by a climatic conference called by the Canadian Government in June 1988. There is now a consensus among the scientific community that, unless urgent action is taken immediately, the world faces disaster on an unprecedented scale in the lifetime of the young people of today.

This present decade has seen the four warmest years of this century and such evidence as we have indicates that 1990 will follow in this trend. Climatologists are also in agreement that weather systems will go to extremes when big changes take place so, while some areas will experience distinct warming, others may experience freak weather which may falsely indicate the reverse. There is strong evidence to the effect that the greatest warming will take place in the Arctic regions with potentially disastrous effects on the water levels throughout the world. The air movements which determine our weather patterns are created by heat. Effects of warming that have already been discerned and studied on a scientific basis include the increasing rate of erosion that has taken place in over three-quarters of the world's beaches. American scientists have detected that the Arctic permafrost has increased its temperatures by over four degrees and research at Cambridge has shown that British plant life and trees have begun to change as a result of the greenhouse effect.

The threat to the world's food supplies comes from the carbon dioxide levels themselves and is not simply restricted to their cataclysmic consequences. Studies at the University of East Anglia have shown that dramatic changes take place in the growth patterns of our major edible plants, and of their natural competitors, the weeds. The comparative capacity to grow and survive is tilted sharply in favour of the weeds. Protein content of food plants declines sharply with increasing levels of atmospheric carbon dioxide – the outlook is bleak indeed.

The threat comes not only from the general level of warming of the atmosphere, and hence of the earth itself, but also from the rapid speed with which this effect is taking place. Core samples taken from the mud on the ocean floor demonstrate a 'trigger effect' in previous climatic changes. At first there is a gradual change then, at some critical point, sudden massive change takes place which completely alters the entire climatic system. In such a way our last ice age was precipitated with devastating suddenness, fatal for much of the animal life of the time. In this way the climate which has allowed our developed civilization to grow and flourish is now under severe threat from the actions of the inhabitants of that very civilization itself. Man is destroying the climate upon which the crops, livestock and his own civilization depends.

The expected timescale in which the full scale of the greenhouse effect will take place is estimated to be over the next forty years. Humanity itself will find it hard to adapt to this rapid change. It will find it even harder if Dr Mostapha Tolba, Director of the United Nations Environmental Programme, is to be believed. Dr Tolba estimates that the rate of change will be ten times faster than the maximum rate the eco-systems can stand. How will man survive without the ecology? Will damage to the living ecology be the only result? What of the environment in general or the earth as a whole? He continues:

A Global sense of urgency is developing. The public concern over global warming is mounting at an unprecedented speed . . . Political leaders now accept the broad scientific consensus that human activity is altering climate and the changes and their impacts will become more pronounced over the next few decades. The warming warning is being heeded.

There are about 4,000 days left in this century. But the scale of the challenge before us means that we shall all need to work, in one way and another, on every day of the coming decade if we are to meet these challenges.

Comments such as these, reinforced by the joint statement of the Secretary General of the United Nations, Javier Perez de Cuellar, and the Norwegian Prime Minister, Gro Harlem Bruntland, explain the sense of urgency now being expressed even by the British Government. The joint statement spoke of the goals that need to be achieved in order to counteract the greenhouse effect, and said:

> To achieve these goals a new Global ethic is needed based on equity, accountability and human solidarity – solidarity with present and future generations – rather than on the tyranny of the immediate.

Vital steps towards reaching this 'new global ethic' have hopefully already begun. In this new age of 'glasnost' the USSR and their old arch rivals the United States have been working together for some years to bring about greater understanding of, and concerted international action to counteract, the greenhouse effect. President Reagan and First Secretary Mikhail Gorbachev signed their first agreement to co-operate in the preservation of the environment. They took this attitude several steps further at subsequent meetings, agreeing to pursue joint studies in global climate and environmental change. They have also co-operated on a study to lessen gas emissions and to use space exploration to study climatic changes on the planet. As these two large and powerful industrial giants are between them the two greatest producers of greenhouse gases let us hope that their joint agreements translate into urgent and effective action.

The battle against the greenhouse effect is not being left solely to the big battalions such as the large powers or smaller nations. There have been some industries that have responded in a positive and responsible manner. One example among many must suffice to show this. A company called Applied Energy Systems from Arlington, Virginia has arranged with aid agencies and the Government of Guatemala to plant 15 million trees. This was the amount calculated to be necessary to absorb the annual output of carbon dioxide from their generating operation. Actions like these must continue to be taken. We cannot afford to wait for disaster to strike before initiating remedial action. As William Feather remarked in *The Business of Life*: 'conditions are never just right. People who delay action until all factors are favourable are the kind who do nothing.'

To understand the full impact of the disasters that can happen to the entire planet as a result of the greenhouse effect is frankly not merely beyond the comprehension of the authors of this book, but in all probability of the scientific community as a whole. They have made some predictions of the possible consequences in addition to those we have already mentioned. Rising sea levels are the most likely result, particularly if the temperature rise is in the order of the probable estimate of three degrees. The scientific consensus is that with a rise in temperature of this level, the resulting rise in water levels as a consequence of polar ice melting would be in the range of eight inches to four and a half feet. If this is true then the world would not only lose many of its centres of population affecting tens of millions of people, but also would lose the vast majority of the vital grain-growing areas on which the survival of the peoples of the world depends. If the warming is enough to melt the West Antarctic ice sheet, a notoriously unstable feature of that region, the projected rise in water levels is estimated to be a truly apocalyptic twenty-six feet.

The flooding is not the only result anticipated by the learned scientists who have studied this matter; the more damaging consequences include massive changes to the weather systems and the ocean currents, the full results of which are truly incalculable. The hurricane 'Gilbert', a rare category 5 hurricane, devastated Jamaica, other Caribbean islands, and the coasts of Mexico and Texas. This hurricane, and its successor, 'Joan', were both ascribed to the greenhouse effect by the scientists and meteorologists who studied them. The most disturbing conclusion of all was reached in a study published by the World Resources

Institute in Washington which claims that, even if there is a determined attempt to ward off the greenhouse effect and such efforts were successful, they would only succeed in postponing the inevitable for perhaps thirty to sixty years.

In view of this pessimistic consensus, what response can mankind make that will enable him to cope with and understand the true nature of the challenge that now faces the planet? Perhaps we should take note of the warning issued by Gro Harlem Bruntland, Prime Minister of Norway:

> We have come to a threshold. If we cross this threshold, we may not be able to return. Will we devote our abilities, our energy and our efforts to further short-term material well-being, or will we commit ourselves to life on earth?

185

SECTION 5

GATHERING AT THE THRESHOLD

The Aquarian Age Takes Root

And I said to the man who stood at the gate of the year:
'Give me a light that I may travel safely into the unknown.'
And he replied:
'Go out into the darkness and put your hand into the hand
of God. That shall be to you better than light and safer than a
known way.'

'The Desert': M. Louise Haskins

The spiritual steps described earlier lead across a threshold, beyond which our perceptions of spiritual and physical reality undergo profound change. We cross such a threshold whole and entire, taking with us what we are. What Pierre Teilhard de Chardin describes as 'the withiness' of things, becomes as real as their physical existence. Our inner perceptions no longer delude us that what goes on inside us doesn't matter as long as our behaviour is socially acceptable. Realities of our inner life are experienced as an integral and powerful constituent of life itself, as part of the entire universe. These spiritual forces are already at work within mankind and can be clearly discerned – if one knows where to look – in many aspects of modern life. This is no accident.

CHAPTER FOURTEEN

THE ROAD LESS TRAVELLED, 'SAFER THAN A KNOWN WAY'

Spiritual or mystical experience is the mirror image of science – a direct perception of nature's unity, the inside of the mysteries that science tries valiantly to know from the outside. This way of understanding pre-dates science by thousands of years. Long before humankind had tools like quantum logic to describe events that ordinary reason could not grasp, individuals moved into the realm of paradox through a shift in consciousness. And there they know that what cannot be *is*. Millions living today have experienced transcendent aspects of reality and have incorporated this knowledge into their lives. A mystical experience, however brief, is validating for those attracted to the spiritual search. The mind now knows what the heart had only hoped for. But the same experience can be deeply distressing to one unprepared for it, who must then try to fit it into an inadequate belief system. Inexorably, direct experience of a larger reality demands that we change our lives.

The Aquarian Conspiracy: Marilyn Ferguson

We are in a very exciting moment in history, perhaps a turning point, stress and perturbations can thrust us into a new and higher order ... Science is proving the reality of a deep cultural vision.

Ilya Prigogine, Nobel Laureate

Disasters and crises throughout history have provided the necessary stimulus for mankind to overcome his natural inertia and seek new ways of transforming adversity to advantage. Ilya Prigogine in his Nobel prize-winning theory on transformations confirmed this when he said: 'science is proving the reality of a deep cultural vision'. The early Platonic fathers and the poets and philosophers of later centuries had a deep and perceptive insight into the fact that nature is a conscious entity within an open, creative universe.

The transcendent powers of nature consciously create the means for human transformation which has been recognized by poets and philosophers throughout the ages.

Two of the poets and philosphers we have mentioned in this book, Goethe and Soloviev, both had world conceptions in which the earth itself was considered to be a living organism of which mankind was an integral part. For Goethe, the 'Idea' of the earth was man. That is to say that man was the central idea of the whole evolution of the earth. While Soloviev, inspired by a deep Russian mysticism and the training of a scientist, stated in his *Philosophy of the Organic* that the earth as a living organism was the Body of Christ. And that the cosmic Christ became the Spirit of the Planet at the moment that the blood flowed from the thrust of the Spear of Longinus on to the earth. Both of these conceptions accept as implicit the fact of a spiritual reality that underpins the physical reality studied by scientists, the same physical reality that is tangible to you or I.

The spiritual reality which fashions, informs and sustains man and the natural world was directly perceptible to the leading Platonists among the Chartres Masters. We have already described at length how they anticipated the coming events described in the Revelation by building the hidden configuration of the Apocalypse in Stone. The symbolism of the 'wounded brain' reveals how they saw the inevitability of the plunge into materialism which would last some five hundred years while mankind experienced an isolation from the spirit which is a pre-requisite for love.

Like Lord Sinclair, the Rosicrucian master who founded Rosslyn, they beheld the period in which mankind would gradually bring materialistic science and technology to birth. But at the same time the Chartres Masters foresaw the re-emergence of their own spiritual faculties as a potential gift for all humanity in the twentieth century, when both rational mind and spiritual perception would merge. It is in this way that the unity of the left and right hemispheres of the brain is achieved through which the soul of man becomes the bridge between two worlds, the spiritual and the terrestrial.

These new spiritual faculties first reappeared in Goethe who was both a poet and a scientist. He illustrates his awe and wonder on perceiving the new spiritual reality in the lines of dedication to his world famous *Faust*:

> Again ye come, ye hovering Forms! I find you
> As early to my clouded sight ye shone!
> Shall I attempt, this once, to seize and bind you?
> Still o'er my heart is that illusion thrown?
> Ye crowd more near! Well then, be power assigned you
> to sway me from your misty, shadowy zone!
> My bosom thrills by youthful passion shaken
> that magic breezes round your march awaken.

Goethe conceived that nature had two separate and distinct boundaries: one leading into a submaterial 'atomic' world in which the intelligent design in the universe could never be found; the other in which Nature herself became a chalice for the spirit which designed, informed and upheld it. Goethe was the first to develop in a scientific way the faculties of Imaginative Cognition, Inspiration and Intuition. Quite apart from his poetic work, he left unpublished manuscripts and personal diaries which to some extent reveal a lifetime study of what is now known as Holistic

190

Science. Rudolf Steiner was chosen to edit these unpublished manuscripts and diaries at the Goethe archives in Weimar. And in this manner it became Steiner's personal destiny to earn his living for a period of fourteen years and establish his academic reputation at the very work which was itself demanded by his own path of inner spiritual development. All those years while he edited Goethe's scientific writings, he was developing in secret his own spiritual faculties to an ever higher degree. It was not until he reached the age of forty-five that he began to make public a new path to spiritual knowledge which he called 'Spiritual Science'. He claimed that he always approached supersensible realities as a scientist and this is why he called his methods of investigation Spiritual Science.

He maintained that it is not sufficient today to reveal the facts of spiritual reality by simply recounting the great inspired teachings of the past, but that the time has come when individuals should begin to advance to a direct knowledge of the supersensible world, by developing their latent faculties in full rational consciousness.

The development, in the last three centuries, of logical thinking and the scientific spirit of observation, was a necessary step in human evolution towards man's discovery, at a higher level, of the spirit background of the universe. His only quarrel with science was that it accepted the limitation of scientific observation to the phenomena of sense existence, and that, in forming its concepts, it regarded the atomistic basis of matter, rather than the forms of physical objects seen in relationship to their environment and their particular metamorphoses, as the key to ultimate knowledge, and took refuge in theoretical concepts, unverifiable by direct observation. He regarded it as fundamental that spiritual knowledge should be justified before the scientific way of thought.

Rudolf Steiner's new way of initiation falls, like its

ancient counterpart, into three stages: Probation, Illumination and Initiation. It also ascends in three phases of spiritual perception: Imagination, Inspiration and Intuition. Imaginative Cognition opens up the vision of the spiritual background of the physical world; Inspiration unveils the macrocosm, giving an understanding of its conditions and of the hierarchies of spiritual beings who inhabit it; Intuition enables man himself to become a full citizen of the spirit world and gives him the means both to act within it and to communicate with all grades of spiritual beings. We have already described these faculties in an earlier chapter relating to the Seals, Trumpets and Vials of the Revelation.

This twentieth-century initiate fulfilled his destiny in revealing to the public how the individual could develop his own spiritual faculties in an objective and scientific manner. Many of his pupils, too numerous to mention here individually by name, explored various aspects of science, medicine, education, agriculture, nutrition and all aspects of health. Steiner's great contribution was the remarkable freedom he gave to those who chose to tread his way of initiation. In retrospect it seems that the very spirit of the time spoke through him, calling to the individual to seek to understand his own destiny by following the path to his own personal spiritual development.

Obviously he was not alone in his efforts to awaken individuals to their own spiritual identity through which they might come to know the spirit in the universe. The moment has at last arrived when mankind as a whole standing at the threshold should awaken to the realities of the spiritual world. Yet this awakening is in the hands of each individual soul:

Thank God our time is now
When wrong comes up to meet
us everywhere

Never to leave us till we take
The greatest stride of soul
Men ever took.
Affairs now are soul size
The enterprise
Is exploration unto God.
Where are you making for?
It takes so many thousand years
to wake.
But will you wake
For pity's sake?

A Sleep of Prisoners: Christopher Fry

In fact, Marilyn Ferguson's *The Aquarian Conspiracy* demonstrates just this incredible rising tide of individuals treading their own separate paths towards spiritual enlightenment. What Bernard Levin describes as 'the aching void' is now part of mankind's universal experience. Levin, a noted journalist, writer and broadcaster, remarking on the crowd of nearly ninety thousand who attended the 1978 'Festival of Mind and Body' in London:

What the world lives by at the moment just will not do. Nor will it; nor do many people at the moment suppose any longer that it will. Countries like ours are full of people who have all the material comforts they desire, yet lead lives of quiet (and at some times noisy) desperation, understanding nothing but the fact that there is a hole inside them and however much food and drink they pour into it, however many motor cars and television sets they stuff it with, however many well-balanced children and loyal friends they parade around the edges of it ... it aches.

Those who attend the festival are seeking something – not certainty, but understanding: understanding of themselves. Almost every path on view starts in the same place, inside the seeker.

The question is being asked more insistently today than

ever before in all history ... The crowds pouring in the turn-stiles at Olympia are only the first drop in a wave that must soon crash over politicians and ideologues and drown their empty claims fathoms deep in a self confidēnce born of a true understanding of their own natures.

It is as though millions of individuals separately have received an awakening call which has started them on their own personal path to self knowledge which slowly begins to reveal the meaning of their lives as human beings and unveils the particular path of personal destiny which they must tread. This is a call that is beyond family, nation, creed, race and gender – a call which transforms the soul into a chalice for the recovery of the individual human spirit.

The call to this spiritual quest has been heard by people from all professions and walks of life, throughout the world. Individuals heed this call in an endless number of different ways as varied as the background of the individuals themselves. In this respect Laurens van der Post believed that the Holy Spirit is at work within humanity itself and is not in any way the exclusive prerogative of the Church. Perhaps the most obvious form this has taken is in the way the Holy Spirit has inspired both the peoples and the leaders of the USSR to bring about 'perestroika' and 'glasnost'. This movement for political change exhibits all the painful signs of spiritual growth one would associate with a sudden change from the rigidity of a dictatorial system into a democratic one. What other explanation can exist but the spiritual? The present leader Mikhail Gorbachev was selected by the same tired and evil system that produced Stalin, Leonid Brezhnev and Yuri Andropov, yet now for politically inexplicable reasons a change occurs of immense intensity – is this not a truly spiritual change?

Millions of individual people worldwide have set out to

find spiritual enlightenment by many varied routes. In a majority of cases they take their first steps along this path totally unaware that it is a spiritual path at all. The entry points to it tend to reflect the varying interests of these new pilgrims of the modern age and can range from the religious to the political.

The reawakening of interest in many of the sects of the Christian faith has been clearly seen in the activities of the television evangelist and, while many of their new flock gain sincere comfort from this novel form of preaching, one is often left with the disturbing thought that yet another means has been found to manipulate sincere believers with the age-old tools of fear and faith by some preachers whose public statements sound more like those of the money changers in the Temple than the words of Jesus Christ himself.

Manipulative 'brainwashing' techniques in the name of religion are not the exclusive preserve of certain Christian Churches, other even more dubious and damaging sects have taken advantage of the vast hunger for spiritual fulfilment that has been growing for over three decades. The main impulse towards renewed spiritual understanding, however, impels most modern pilgrims of the new Aquarian age along non-religious pathways.

Concern for the environment, worries about pollution and the survival of the very planet itself have inspired people to question previously accepted values. The desire for good personal health, the decline in social cohesion and loss of faith in the political system have also made a significant contribution to the large, growing army of men and women who are no longer satisfied with being told what to think, and who wish to exercise their right to question and think for themselves, reaching beyond the limits of material knowledge and accepting the existence of the supersensible. Accepting and enjoying the scientific, technological and

195

medical achievements of recent decades has not filled the 'aching void' of which Bernard Levin spoke so eloquently – on the contrary the very marvels of the material world highlight the spiritual vacuum at the heart of modern life in the twentieth century.

This quest for spiritual reality and meaning has been growing steadily since the early years of this century. Some movements and groups inspired many individuals to continue their search on a personal basis, sustained in many instances by the obvious benefits they gained from the so-called 'alternative sciences', especially medicine, and encouraged by their growing perception of the reality of a spiritual entity that guided and sustained the material world that could be seen, touched and felt.

After a period of sustained and quiet growth, this amorphous movement, a collection of dedicated individuals who scorned hierarchical structures, experienced a period of intense growth in the early sixties. The epicentre of this intense and explosive period of growth was the state of California in the USA, but on a smaller scale it was repeated throughout the developed world. Dissatisfied by the impersonal complexities of the modern world, people began to search for meaning and a sense of personal identity in a society that regarded them as mere cyphers to be satisfied by the provision of material goods.

Many routes were taken on this search, not all particularly relevant to the real meaning of personal destiny, but as fashions changed and the bogus nature of what many self-appointed gurus had to offer became apparent, the majority of our new pilgrims found that they were all on the same path, irrespective of their starting point. A path that led through a discipline of personal discovery to the very threshold of the spiritual world.

Certain unifying themes and shared experiences unite this motley throng, a growing certainty about the unseen

196

spiritual reality that guides all terrestrial events, and a deepening awareness that we can all learn to live in harmony with the earth – not exploiting and despoiling it. Above all, a sustained ability actually to learn to live by the principles of love and mutual respect became the discernible hallmark of the modern spiritual novice.

The individuals following the path that leads inevitably to the unveiling of their personal destiny and the threshold of the spiritual world do not act as part of an organized movement, despite their common goals and achievements. They still remain distinct, separate, individual people, united from time to time by their interest but treading their own personal path. The form of communication they use to keep informed of current developments is called networking; this permits knowledge of events, seminars and festivals to be circulated in an informal but highly efficient way. Centres of some excellence do exist which stimulate and guide the novices to the subsequent steps on the path to modern initiation, but all is achieved informally and in a spirit of gentleness that respects and preserves the individual spiritual identity of each person. Essalin in California is perhaps the best known of these centres, but they do exist world wide.

A look at the shelves of any so-called alternative bookshop situated anywhere in Europe or across America or even Australia will give the reader some idea of the enormous number of different approaches to the path of self discovery. It is also clear that these approaches are highly individual and do not have a place in any hierarchical system. Indeed the dangers of manipulation are much more apparent in the fundamentalist attitude in both the Christian and the Muslim worlds. The only danger that may be present for the individual on this search lies in the possibility of economic exploitation by some materialistically minded gurus who seem more intent in gathering golden

Rolls-Royces than genuinely promoting spiritual awareness amidst their blind, orange-robed followers.

Throughout this book we have been presenting above all else a single theme regarding the meaning of the Spear of Destiny in this apocalyptic age. How the understanding of the history and the powers associated with the Spear of Longinus leads the individual soul towards both self knowledge and a true insight into the meaning of personal destiny. We believe that the Spear will become the accepted symbol of those millions who are rallying as representatives of the individual human spirit all over the globe.

It is the Spirit of the Time, the *Zeitgeist*, whom we have described as the beneficent spirit of the Spear, that weaves the separate strands of the destinies of millions of individuals into the fabric of resistance to the working of the twofold face of evil. To these individuals the coming catastrophes foretold by St John are nature's reply to the blind exploitation by mankind of the world we live in. Those on a spiritual path will perceive a meaning behind nature's transformative powers, accepting nature as a powerful ally and not a disinterested power to be feared and somehow subdued. Using the powers and faculties of the spirit we discern how physical adversity can be transformed to spiritual advantage.

Such a knowledge was known to the people of ancient times who felt themselves to be part of 'Mother Earth', a concept which was an integral part of ancient civilizations who experienced the soul of the earth with an atavistic immediacy. As we have already described, the concept of the world soul reappeared within the Christian community of the Chartres Masters who dedicated their work to the Goddess Natura. They believed at the same time that the Virgin Mary, whose effigy was for the first time carved in stone on the porticoes of their cathedrals, was an earthly incarnation. The same theme recurs in all the major

Marian apparitions. The spiritual perception that granted this conception has been lost to mankind with the descent of consciousness to its present scientific rational state, but with the reappearance of spiritual faculties that have emerged with the unification of right and left brain thinking, the concept of 'Gaia', the world soul, has become more universally recognized by all those who tread spiritual paths.

It is with the same emerging faculties that mankind will experience what St Luke describes as 'The Son of Man coming in a cloud with power and great glory'. The vision of the Etheric Christ, an event which people from many different faiths have already experienced this century, is the result of the re-emergence of spiritual faculties. The spiritual reality that lies behind these visions is the fact that the living Christ has never left us. Meister Eckhart, the great German mystic, told his flock that they should not expect to see God with the physical eye as they see a cow in a field. It is only with spiritual faculties that the human soul can behold the living Christ. This progressive process in which more and more human beings will have a direct experience of the presence of God will become widespread at the troubled times of the global catastrophes when He will reveal himself even to large gatherings. The tragedy is that this so-called 'second coming' has been misinterpreted as another appearance of Christ in the flesh. Already the true vision has been shared by a large number of people from all walks of life and from many nations, but most people have been reluctant to speak of such an intimate and direct spiritual meeting. As time passes, this mystery of the direct presence of Jesus Christ will rest at the heart of all those who belong to 'The Aquarian Conspiracy'.

It would be naive to believe that 'The Aquarian Conspiracy' is the only conspiracy; there are of course others of a sinister nature. A close look at the fabric of contemporary events reveals their presence. As we have already amply demonstrated, there have always been occult lodges on earth directly concerned with serving the evil. This was particularly obvious at the time when Jesus Christ was on earth. The dual face of evil that sought to tempt him in the wilderness was also working quite directly through the Sanhedrin, the Pharisees and the Sadducees who sought time and again to trap him so that they might put him to death. The only reported occasion when Jesus showed his wrath and physically confronted the established order was when he turned over the tables of the money changers in the Temple. In this direct way he struck at the very source of the political power of Annas and Caiaphas, the high priests.

The Romans, who regarded their own pantheon of gods as supreme, forced subjugated peoples to pay for their religious sacrifices in Roman coinage. Annas and Caiaphas ran the money-changing operation in the Temple at immense profit, exploiting the religious fervour of the simple people who came to worship, by controlling the exchange rate. The Sadducees were not only a priestly order, but also black adepts of the highest degree who were even prepared to crucify their Messiah rather than lose their power over the people. Such occult lodges who serve the evil powers have continued to exist through two thousand years of Christendom. We have illustrated how such an occult grouping inspired the Academy of Jundi-Shapur where they were taught directly by Behemoth, the beast of 666. Such a central lodge in the service of the evil exists on the earth today and has been making its preparations for the prophesied appearance of the Anti-Christ.

It was out of such insight into the working of evil that Thomas Campbell was inspired to write: 'Coming events cast their shadow before'. With just such a perception of the working of evil powers behind the changing scenes of the time, we revealed the real significance of the whole series of events which led up to the appearance of the Leviathan in Adolf Hitler and the whole continuing conspiracy of those souls who helped to bring him to power and set him on his course to world conquest.

The drama and symbolism of the Nazi era came about through the machinations of evil powers and the interweaving of the destinies of the souls that served them. But first the invisible hand of the evil was at work within the general milieu of social, cultural, financial, industrial and political structures and interwoven with perverted racial, religious and atavistic tendencies in the German people in order to create that alien civilization which brought about the Holocaust. *The Spear of Destiny*, Part I, revealed a thread of black occult initiates who were indispensable to the rise of Hitler. The same process is at work today. Learn where to look for it and you will most surely perceive the effect it is having on contemporary events.

An international occult lodge is secretly at work in the heart of the financial world which spreads its malign influence throughout the political and economic structures of the entire planet. Total control of the political machinery of all parties is sought, by infiltrating and financing not only the majority of candidates from all sides, but also by the provision of economic advisers to governments. The tentacles of such an international occult circle reach into the intelligence systems and the media, into education, science and the military.

The stage has been reached now in which many organizations with wholly admirable and benevolent aims may soon become the vehicles through which the twofold face of evil achieves its further and progressive aims. In order to bring about the world dictatorship prophesied by St John, what better organizations can the evil powers subvert than those laudable pillars of modern civilization which are

201

dedicated to world peace and international cooperation – the United Nations and the movements towards international federation such as the EEC, the Organization of African States and the Pan American movement.

SECTION 6

THE PROPHESIED FUTURE

Nightmare or Reality?

CHAPTER FIFTEEN

THE MARK OF THE BEAST, THE GREAT DICTATOR AND THE ANTI-CHRIST

We must eradicate from our souls all fear and terror of what comes towards man out of the future ... We must look forward with absolute equanimity to all that may come and we must think only that whatever comes is given to us by a world direction that is full of wisdom.

Rudolf Steiner (from an unpublished lecture
'Death and Immortality in the Light of Spiritual
Science' delivered in Bremen, 12 November 1911)

The structure of the Revelation, in so far as it is related to our own time, pivots upon 666: the number of the Beast. There has been a lasting occult tradition that Ahriman, the figure of the Anti-Christ, will be born in the year 1998, a number which is a multiple of 666. The actual date in which this spirit of materialism sought to manifest himself in order to teach the lodge of adepts in Jundi-Shapur was the year 666. As we have described, this attempt to take over the earth was frustrated by the rise of Islam and the arrival of the wild, primitive and fanatical tribesmen at the Academy in Persia beneath the Afghan foothills. If the impulse of Behemoth had succeeded in Jundi-Shapur, Christianity would have been bypassed and replaced by an all-pervasive materialism.

When the second multiple of 666 occurred in history in AD 1332, the sun demon Sorath, the third of the trinity of evil, inspired the torture and the burning of the leading Knights Templar by working through the possessed soul of

Philip the Bel, the King of France. Outwardly Philip the Fair was driven to use these extremes of torture to gain false confessions from the Templars and justify his theft of the immense gold store of the Order. Inwardly the French King was possessed by the sun demon who was determined to defeat by black magic the spiritual aims of the Templars who sought a truly Christian development of the European continent.

The third multiple of 666 will take place in 1998 when the fallen Seraphim, Ahriman, the very spirit of materialism will incarnate in the flesh personally to direct the total destruction of the spiritual aims of Christianity. The following thirty years of the twenty-first century will see the mighty confrontation between good and evil in the battle for the planet. And it is within this time framework between now and the end of the third decade of the next century that St John predicts a tremendous sequence of apocalyptic events beginning with the great catastrophes the ancient seer of Patmos so clearly prophesied.

A whole number of psychics through the centuries, even as far back as Nostradamus, have also predicted the coming catastrophes. One of the best-known modern psychics was Edgar Cayce, an American who died in 1945 at the age of sixty-seven. Cayce, a non-denominational Christian, who had extraordinary transcendent powers of diagnosis and healing, claimed to read past and future events from the Akashic record. His vision in this respect reached as far back as ancient Atlantis and the great water catastrophes which destroyed it. Looking into the future he predicted catastrophes which would take place towards the end of the twentieth century, including tremendous earthquakes on the west coast of America, especially in Los Angeles and San Francisco, and also disastrous earth movements on the east coast which would totally destroy Manhattan. He described how the greater part of Japan would disappear under the sea after major earth movements in that area. He also prophesied the tilting of the earth's axis in the year 2000. However, some of the disasters predicted by Cayce, including a major catastrophe in Florida and the Bahamas which he foresaw as taking place in the seventies and eighties, simply did not happen in the timescale he predicted. They did not happen at all.

Very large numbers of people from all walks of life have had dreams or visions of coming catastrophes. The question is: what are they really experiencing? Is it a manifestation of the sub-conscious layers of fear which have gripped humanity in the present apocalyptic century? Trevor Ravenscroft has had such visions in which tremendous earthquakes and tidal waves have wrought destruction, the earth and sea turning red, enormous towering columns of water spreading across the ocean and fissures opening as the result of huge earth movements. But not for one minute does he believe that he was perceiving coming catastrophes, but only a projection of the collective unconscious fears of mankind. The trained and objective perception of spiritual initiates is of a different order from involuntary psychic vision, which more often than not has no reality.

The Platonic school at Chartres in the Middle Ages, a secret centre of profound Christian initiation, developed in its pupils just such a disciplined and directed spiritual perception. As we have described in an earlier chapter, it was the Platonic initiates of Chartres who conceived the apocalyptic configuration in stone which included the alignment of seven cathedrals between the two Pillars of Wisdom and Strength at Cintra and Rosslyn. The whole configuration under the arch of the Milky Way was built to symbolize the new Jerusalem of the Revelation in which the planet was seen as the body of Christ, the Earth Spirit who progressively permeates all nature.

The very sacraments themselves were for these Platonic fathers the sign that Christ permeates and transforms all earthly matter with his being. And they anticipated that a historical moment would arise in this progressive process which they called the 'Transfiguration of the Earth'. This process will take the outward form of the emission of pure light from every aspect of nature. It is predicted that this will occur shortly before the great disasters prophesied by St John in the Revelation. This prophecy was apparently confirmed in this century during one of the Marian apparitions in Europe. On 18 June 1961, in the Spanish village of San Sebastian de Garabandal, a series of apparitions began for a small group of young peasant girls. Over two thousand such apparitions were recorded by these children, and among them was confirmation not only of the coming great disasters but also of an 'event of light'. 'Everything in the world would emit light for a short period of time.' This event would do no harm but would serve as a portent of disaster.

The whole of the Apocalypse advances entirely in rhythms of seven – The Seven Stars, The Seven Golden Candlesticks, The Seven Angels, The Seven Messages to the Seven Churches, The Seven Seals, Trumpets and Vials of Wrath follow each other in succession. The same seven-foldness was built into the Apocalypse in Stone by the initiated fathers of Chartres and those that followed them. The Seven Stars represent the Seven Planets and, as we have already described, the Seven Cathedrals were built upon the Seven Sacred Planetary Sites. When the alignment of planets in the heavens is exactly similar to the planetary alignment of the seven cathedrals on the earth below, the moment is ripe for the transfiguration of the earth which is to precede the great disasters. There have already been two great planetary alignments in the last two decades, but that alignment which is closest to the earthly alignment of planetary sites will appear in May in the year 2000. This appears to be the date that the Platonic

207

initiates of the Middle Ages were anticipating as the critical turning point of the Apocalypse. They anticipated this and the appearance, prophesied in Revelation 12, of the being to whom their life and work were dedicated, the goddess of Natura whom we speak of today as Gaia, the soul of the world.

> A great and wondrous sign appeared in heaven: a woman clothed with the sun, with the moon under her feet and a crown of twelve stars on her head. She was pregnant and cried out in pain as she was about to give birth.
> Revelation (New International Version): 12, verses 1–2

The Virgin of the Apocalypse, the eternal feminine, is presented as giving birth to a son, the eternal male principal, the individual human spirit which seeks to come to birth in every man in this moment when mankind as a whole stands at the threshold of the spiritual world. The awareness of the human spirit, always a part of the entelechy of man, has been removed through the gradual process of materialism which has all but annihilated the awareness of the soul itself. Now at this turning point in the evolution of human consciousness St John presents a heavenly symbolism which calls for a new spiritual awakening. It is at this moment that the culmination of man's rational development will merge with his spiritual perception to initiate a new paradigm.

Rudolf Steiner spent a lifetime building a bridge between the world of the spirit and the world of nature. He discovered a way through which thinking as an instrument of scientific investigation was itself raised to such a level of higher consciousness that it passed the bounds of sense existence and arrived at an objective and rational understanding of the spirit background of the physical world. Nobody in this century has given clearer indications as regards the development of the spirit senses and the spiritual faculties of man. His clairvoyance broke through the barriers of time reaching back into past millennia and forward into a far distant future.

Steiner would not speak publicly about the catastrophes foretold by St John because he did not wish to create a fatalistic and doomsday attitude towards coming events at the end of the century. Yet on occasion, with close pupils and small advanced groups of students, he confirmed that these castastrophes would take place on a global scale. He was reluctant to reveal his knowledge of the coming world disasters in case it discouraged people from concentrating upon the more important issue of individual spiritual growth and development. He disclosed in private conversations that he himself would be back on earth again at the end of the century and that his closer followers would be free to choose whether they too returned to earth with him. 'Can I return with you?' an elderly woman asked him. 'Yes,' said Steiner, 'if you would be willing to walk with me across the rubble of Europe on bare feet.'

Dr Steiner told Walter Johannes Stein, who inspired the writing of *The Spear of Destiny*, that the catastrophes would be global in extent and that in Europe flooding would reach a level beyond the imagination of most people. He spoke of the disappearance of Poland beneath the water and how the Russian frontier in the west would be a coastline stretching from the Baltic to the Black Sea. He also described how the waters of the Rhine would flood even to the top of the foothills of the Jura Mountains. To others he spoke of the destruction of a greater part of England by earth movements and floods. It is important to note here that these descriptions of coming events seen through his objective spiritual vision were given more than sixty years before the full implications of the greenhouse effect were fully understood by the scientific community of today.

A time-frame for the catastrophes emerges when we take into consideration the scientific scenario, the prophecy of St John the Divine, the general indications associated with the Marian apparitions and the objective spiritual perception of Dr Rudolf Steiner, the greatest spiritual initiate of the twentieth century. The scientific assessment suggests a timescale within the range of thirty to forty years at most before the full impact of the greenhouse effect will be seen. Yet it may be earlier, who are we to say? The reports of the Spanish Marian apparition suggest a somewhat shorter period before the 'event of light', which we have interpreted as the Spiritual Transfiguration of the Earth.

A pivotal point that gives a more precise indication concerns the actual date of the physical birth of Ahriman, the Anti-Christ. All genuine occult tradition points to the year 1998, the third multiple of 666 – the number of the beast, When Dr Steiner was asked by Dr Friedrich Rittelmyer if this was indeed the date of the birth of Ahriman, he replied: 'This is the year he is expected to be born but it is a characteristic of Ahriman that he is inclined to act earlier than expected.'

However, Steiner gave indications in various lectures that a build-up of catastrophic events would herald the birth of the great tempter of mankind and that such disasters could take the form of earthquakes, famines, pestilences and floods. It could be argued with some force that these have already occurred only review the events of the last few years and we discover the eruption of Mount St Helens, the serious earthquakes in Greece, Nicaragua, Turkey and Mexico City, the devastating earthquake in Soviet Armenia which alone had a death toll of over one hundred thousand, flooding in the Sudan, in Bangladesh and the Punjab, drought and famine in Africa, widespread drought in the USA, freak weather conditions such as 'Hurricane Gilbert' which destroyed vast tracts in the Caribbean, Central

America and parts of the United States, and finally the AIDS epidemic which is taking such a horrendous toll worldwide.

One must not forget that Ahriman is the spirit of dissemblance, the deceiver, but one thing is certain – when he does incarnate into a mortal human body he will be bound by the same life span as all other human beings. And this above all gives us a time frame for the world's recovery from the coming catastrophes. For Ahriman will declare himself as the re-appearance of Jesus Christ in the flesh around his thirtieth year. And this will coincide with the emergence of the Great Dictator at the peak of his world power. This would give us a time frame of the next forty years for the turning point of those critical events predicted in the Revelation for our time.

We cannot predict with absolute accuracy the exact date on which the great global disasters prophesied by St John will take place, but all the evidence we have seen leads us to the inevitable conclusion that mankind is genuinely on the brink of experiencing them. Their timing and their extent must be conditioned by mankind's capacity to recover and rebuild world civilization in time for the confrontation with the Anti-Christ and the Great Dictator in the third decade of the twenty-first century.

Civilization as we know it today will almost totally disappear as a result of these great global disasters which will be more intense and destructive than anything in the recorded history of the planet. According to the Revelation, one-third of the population of the earth will die in the disasters which St John predicts with such insistence. And this alone must give us some measure of the destruction which is about to take place and the formidable conditions of the immediate aftermath. At the same time we must consider man's capacity to recover which at this time is even greater than it was in the aftermath of the first great apocalyptic

211

phase of the Hitler war which left most of Europe in ruins.

The conditions after the catastrophes have occurred will vary enormously from continent to continent, nation to nation and place to place. Some landscapes as we now know them will disappear altogether, many will be altered beyond recognition, others will be relatively unscathed. New seas will appear, rivers will change course or disappear and new or enlarged land masses will emerge. How much immediate warning of these events will be given is not known. What can be deduced however is that the surviving populations will be faced with chaos on a global scale.

Mankind's capacity to recover from localized or even continent-wide destruction is a matter of historical fact; many of the problems that the survivors will face can be deduced from past and recent events, such as the widespread devastation in Armenia. Famine, pestilence, and the need for warmth and shelter will be the foremost problems people will face, the inevitable consequence of the mass scramble for the few remaining resources will be a total breakdown of law and order. Unlike the recovery in Europe in the aftermath of the Second World War, there will be no immediate aid forthcoming from outside sources.

Amid the ruins of the worst-affected areas, people will be bereft of food, shelter, power supplies and all the amenities that we at present take for granted. There will be no hospitals and medical services to cope with the epidemics of water-borne diseases such as cholera, typhoid and paratyphoid that will decimate the enfeebled survivors. All forms of communication will cease. Lack of oil will stop all transport, lack of power will render today's sophisticated communication systems useless. Roads and bridges will be swept away and mankind will face the problems of the early Middle Ages or worse, leaving localized pockets of survivors to fend for themselves. Those who can will take to arms to defend their few meagre possessions or to take them by force from others. The need for shelter will be paramount, all housing will be destroyed, leaving the survivors to find some way to protect themselves from the extremes of climate and the wandering bands resorting to brigandage. Something of this situation is suggested in the Revelation in the words:

> The sky receded like a scroll, rolling up, and every mountain and island was removed from its place. Then the kings of the earth, the princes, the generals, the rich, the mighty, and every slave and every free man hid in caves among the rocks of the mountains.
> Revelation (New International Version):6, verses 14–15

Civilization in some parts of the world will be relatively unaffected. For instance in the north east of the United States of America the damage may not be so considerable in the inland areas of New England and even as far south as Virginia. On other continents similar large areas may also be spared from the worst effects of the disasters. Whole cities sometimes several neighbouring cities with their hinterlands intact and unharmed, will still function as before with a political and administrative structure unchanged. Law and order, perhaps with the help of the presence of the army, will be maintained. The entire surviving structure will facilitate food rationing, some semblance of power supplies and a limited capacity for transport and communication. Total dedication to one single aim will be the overwhelming priority of the government of these areas, to ensure the survival and recovery of its inhabitants. Martial law, enforced and directed labour and the suspension of democratic rights are the means by which these objectives will be reached. All citizens, irrespective of their previous political beliefs, will willingly co-operate with and support this 'New Order'.

Civil administrations today throughout the developed world have plans to cope with massive disasters, combining the expertise of civil servants, police, army and rescue services. International ability to co-operate in giving some effective relief has been repeatedly seen in territories as far apart and as inaccessible as Ethiopia, the Sudan, Bangladesh, the Punjab and the mountainous regions of Soviet Armenia. In the initial phase after the disasters in those areas that survive with little damage, these plans will come into effect. The controlling factor in how the recovery will progress is the access to fuel and power supplies. Technicians, miners, oilmen and specialized planners will be at a premium and will gain growing political power. The men who have existing experience and great acumen in exploiting these resources will of course be those who already have a proven record of success, the businessmen who own and direct the major corporations. These men will now gain total political control, based not on the ballot box, but on the complete dependence of entire populations on the services they can provide or deny. Logic dictates that this will be so, but it would be foolish to project any form of detailed prognosis based on any other rationale than fundamental human need.

With the growing dependence of our present civilization on modern technology, the importance of fuel and power sources is already well established. The countries and businessmen who control these vital natural resources are in fact the hidden rulers of all the industrialized nations. The great international conglomerates in the oil business are more powerful than most nations. Profits from these operations have enabled the major shareholders to extend their power and control over a wide variety of other essential industries and services such as banking, pharmaceuticals, communications and media and indirectly into the political arena. Amongst this fraternity are groups who for

214

more than fifty years have been seeking a way to create greater international unity and co-operation under a 'New World Order'. Some seek to accomplish this from altruistic and humanitarian motives, others see it as a means to gain greater wealth, power and control.

The gradual recovery of the rest of the world will mainly arise from the spreading influence and power of the areas who not only remained virtually intact but also began to develop the new power structures we have already described. Their influence will extend not by conquest but by their capacity to supply and maintain basic needs in return for acquiescence to the new political order. This process of growing recovery will be mirrored in all parts of the globe where the essential services, power and food supplies have remained intact. Recovery will be enhanced by new technologies that the needs of the time demand. This will further reinforce the control exercised by the new ruling class, people no longer having civil rights, only civil obligations.

The rapid expansion of these recovering areas leads inevitably to greater communication and physical contact between them; in many cases this will be beneficial and lead to the re-emergence of nations. Most nations will be inclined to unite peacefully under the direction of those who seek to create a new world order. Others will be opposed to this as it is in conflict with their own ideology which dictates that they become the world power. Due to the widespread devastation, Europe will be slow to recover, while in Russia recovery will be patchy and slow due to its vast area and the difficulties of communication. Central control in Russia will also be complicated because of the wide diversity of its peoples. This will make Slavonic Russia and Europe particularly vulnerable to the onslaught of China for whom is predicted the fastest recovery of all.

One of the great Saxon Kings, Henry I, a claimant to the

Spear of Destiny, turned back the invasion of the Magyars from the east at the battle of Lech near Vienna. And it was during this period that there arose a prophecy from the lips of a Saxon soothsayer that after a thousand years there would be another invasion by the yellow hordes of the East which would overrun Europe unless it was turned back by the Germanic people. Since that time the threat of a 'yellow peril' has always existed as a kind of nightmare in Europe, made more real by the presence of vast numbers of Mongolian troops within the Russian armies that overran eastern Europe towards the end of the Hitler war. Soloviev, in his writings regarding the prophesies of the Revelation, pictures Europe partly occupied by Mongolian hordes after the great disasters have taken place. Rudolf Steiner, looking into the future with the trained and disciplined eye of a master initiate, described how much of Europe would be occupied for a period by Chinese troops following the global catastrophes. Indeed he described this Chinese occupation in some detail saying that eastern Europe and some parts of central Europe including Germany would be for a time under the martial law of a Chinese army.

The motivation for such an invasion could be quite varied, including such factors as the need to seek sources of food, raw materials and technology. Other reasons would include the imposition of the Chinese ideology on a vulnerable and enfeebled Europe. The controlling factor in the success of such an enterprise would be the vast numbers of Chinese who would survive the catastrophes. After such an event when many of the world's resources have been destroyed, warfare would inevitably revert for a time to a more primitive form, using older weapon systems where force of numbers would be the deciding factor. Even if China lost more than one-third of its present population, there would still remain more than five hundred million Chinese to be reckoned with. No state or continent recovering from catastrophes of the magnitude foretold by St John could possibly resist an invasion by such a force.

Military or diplomatic defeat of an invasion of such magnitude could only be achieved by the emergence of a leader of extraordinary military, diplomatic and organizational skill. The advent on earth of such a leader of genius and unassailable power is foretold in the Revelation which describes the effect his charismatic personality and powers of persuasion will have upon mankind.

> The whole world was astonished and followed the beast . . . He was given power to make war against the saints and to conquer them. And he was given authority over every tribe, people, language and nation. All inhabitants of the earth will worship the beast . . . He who has an ear let him hear . . . If anyone is to go into captivity, into captivity he will go. If anyone is to be killed with the sword, with the sword he will be killed. This calls for patient endurance and faithfulness on the part of the saints.
>
> Revelation (New International Version): 13, verses 3,
> 7–8, 9–10

Only through the understanding that the drama and symbolism of history is the result of the interweaving of reincarnation patterns can we perceive how the emergence of a soul of such a stature as the Great Dictator of the Revelation will become for a period the ruler of the entire world. The idea that such a personality could arise solely as an accident of history can only spring from blinkered and limited perceptions of human destiny. Just as Winston Churchill was the last bead on a thread of previous lives on earth in which he had gained the insight and experience to become the leader of democracy, so the previous incarnations of the Great Dictator have prepared him for his ultimate destiny.

Anybody who has ever given it a thought will not be surprised that this mighty tyrant is the reappearance of the military genius and administrator who rose to power on a 'whiff of grapeshot' during the last days of 'the terror' during the French Revolution. The entire banking, educational and administrative system of Europe bears the imprint of his thinking to this day. Such was the awesome skill and military genius of this man of 'Transcendent Merit' that the entire legal code of western Europe still bears his name – the Code Napoleon.

Napoleon Bonaparte was born in Ajaccio, Corsica, on 15 August 1769, the son of a minor aristocrat of Italian nationality. At his birth he was described by local sooth-sayers as 'the seeming reincarnation of the son of one of the fourteenth-century *Italian Condottiere*'. The soothsayers in this instance were not so far wrong because the child born to the Bonaparte family was the reincarnation of Cesare Borgia, the most feared name of the Italian Renaissance – a man of exceptional brilliance, ambition, military skill and personal bravery, whose ambition is clearly demonstrated by his favourite motto, 'Aut Caesar, aut nihil', either Caesar or nothing. The unscrupulous cunning of Cesare Borgia was immortalized by Machiavelli as 'The Prince' in his major work on despotic leadership.

In every instance of the appearance on earth of this tyrannical soul there have always been predictions at his birth of the greatness of his coming destiny. This was especially the case at the birth of Genghis Khan who united the Mongol tribes into a nation and led their path of conquest to create an empire stretching from the Pacific Ocean to the Adriatic Sea. Only his untimely death stopped the feared 'Temujin', the scourge of God, from conquering the whole of Europe. Shamans stated at his birth that heaven had sent the Mongol tribes a leader with a great destiny. Born at a time when China was in a period of decline, Genghis Khan used the natural abilities of the horsemen of the Mongol tribes to create the world's most feared fighting force, an army whose lightning speed of manoeuvre and utter ruthlessness struck terror into the hearts of the entire world. In his conquered territories, this seeming unschooled tribal horseman displayed extraordinary administrative skills and powers of charismatic leadership.

The innate qualities of leadership and ambition that have manifested themselves in every incarnation of this dictatorial personality soon became obvious in the early career of Napoleon Bonaparte. Promoted to the rank of Brigadier General in charge of the artillery of the Army of Italy, he displayed the very qualities that were to take him to the pinnacle of power and the ultimate domination of all Europe. Turning the under-strength, ill-equipped rabble that constituted the Army of Italy into an efficient, well-motivated fighting machine, Napoleon laid the basis for all his future strategy and success. Speed of manoeuvre, the ability to live off the land, and the promise of loot-a-plenty were the means by which he defeated the professional army of Austria in the Italian campaign. To these qualities he added the unexpected skills of a wily diplomatist. Those territories he did not conquer, he added to the French hegemony by diplomacy and alliance. After his conquests he returned to France and at the age of twenty-five began to show his political skills, gaining appointment as First Consul of France, virtual dictator of the new post-revolutionary nation.

Rising to power as a result of the revolutionary process and believing that political change was both vital and inevitable, Napoleon did not see the need for radical social reform which lay at the very heart of the call for 'Liberté, Égalité, Fraternité'. Displaying an indefatigable capacity for hard work, this man of destiny proceeded on a series of changes that completely transformed the administration of

France. Ever willing to take advice, and using men of talent rather than the high born, Napoleon reformed the educational system, instituting the national curriculum, established the complete independence of the judiciary and commenced the lifelong work that still bears his name – the creation of a system of justice before the law. Yet, despite his personal sense of justice, he was nevertheless responsible for creating the foundations for the modern police state. To protect his own power structure he established a secret police force under the infamous Fouché, which became the most efficient internal intelligence system and a model for the horrendous totalitarian police states of our century.

Despising the masses, he showed charismatic powers of persuasion to successfully manipulate public opinion. Personally indifferent to religion himself, he felt that 'the people needed it' and that it was a useful tool to direct and control populations. Corsica's 'Man of Destiny' has been described as 'the last of the Enlightened Despots' and vividly displayed the very qualities which are anticipated in the life of the Great Dictator. Napoleon's overwhelming ambition for world power which changed the history of France and Europe was frustrated in his lifetime but will be consummated with devastating effect when he becomes ruler of the planet in his coming incarnation as the vessel of the Leviathan and the essential partner to the rise of the Anti-Christ.

Somewhere in the United States of America, growing up as a contemporary of the Great Dictator in Europe, the Anti-Christ will reach maturity. Amongst the immensely rich, powerful and influential families we have already described, there exists an occult lodge which has been consciously anticipating the birth in the flesh of Ahriman. And it is within this fraternity that the successive generations of the Ben Jesu family who masterminded the Academy of Jundi-Shapur have reincarnated. It will be from their bloodline

220

that the great genius of materialism will arise – the most superbly gifted rational mind, the ultimate spirit of technology and the greatest master of occult and black magic gifts. The anticipation of this birth is so widespread in the western world that four major films – the *Omen* series – which lacked any real occult insight into this reality, achieved great commercial success.

The prophesied birth of Jesus was heralded by an angelic annunciation and the appearance of the initiated Kings who followed the star to Bethlehem. So too the birth of Ahriman will be anticipated and attended by initiates of a more sinister order. And the child will be nurtured and protected by the very reincarnated souls who worshipped him as their god in the Academy beneath the foothills of the Afghan mountains. Incarnating around the same time, and perhaps born in the same vicinity, will be those souls who have prepared themselves across the millennia to be his disciples. By the age of twelve years the Anti-Christ will be acclaimed for a mind of immense intellectual power and spiritual gifts. Soloviev states that the mass of humanity will regard him as 'a Lamb', a being of apparent innocence and the deepest spiritual insight bringing a divine message.

The precise means by which he will come to public notice and acclaim is impossible to predict with accuracy. One thing is certain: this mighty and alien spirit, a fallen being from the very highest hierarchies of the spiritual world, will proclaim himself to be the reappearance on earth of Jesus Christ. It is unlikely that he will ever belong to any established church. His entire youth and adolescence may even be as hidden as the early life of Jesus of Nazareth, and his ministry could start at a similar age, during his thirtieth year. On the other hand it would appear more likely that he comes to public notice as a technological genius in all fields of science, especially pharmaceutical science, in which his astonishing gifts may lead to the development and manufacture of new wonder drugs to combat the pestilences and plagues that will occur as a consequence of the great disasters.

Once his ministry commences he will make full use of the new technologies of communication so that the entire world will know of his miraculous deeds at the instant they happen. He will mimic the miracles of Jesus, the blind will see, the lame will walk, the dead will rise again and evil spirits will be cast out from the afflicted. Only those people who have developed their own individual spiritual insight will know that 'The Prince of Demons, he drives out Demons'. He will proclaim that two thousand years ago he had taught mankind in parables. Since then, humanity has matured and developed far enough to receive the teachings of the Son of God in a more direct, sophisticated and scientific way. The unthinking masses will be overpowered by his miraculous deeds while the scientific community will be astonished by the incredible range and depth of his technological and intellectual insight across the entire spectrum of modern science.

Those people who are striving towards spiritual reality and have become aware of the real mystery of the second coming of Christ, will be able to identify Ahriman in the flesh as the Two-Horned Beast. Many among them know that Christ who is the Earth Spirit will not incarnate again in the flesh. For the mass of humanity, especially those with a dogmatic or a fundamentalist attitude, Ahriman will be revered as the returning Christ.

The increasing rate of recovery from the chaos of the global disasters under the leadership and inspiration of Ahriman, who has united science and religion, will create for the first time in history an almost totally unified population. Following the precise words of the gospel, 'Render unto Caesar that which is Caesar's', Ahriman will deliver his entire global flock into the waiting arms of the Great

Dictator of the New World Order, promising a new age of peace and prosperity to mankind.

The New World Order will bring to mankind new freedoms: freedom from starvation, freedom from unemployment, freedom from poverty and freedom from individual responsibility to others in exchange for collective and individual responsibility to the State, obedience to the dictator and belief in the Anti-Christ as God on Earth. The new laws that will underpin the New World Order will appear to reflect all the political slogans of the old, outmoded capitalist and communist systems of the past, which were anyway lateral inversions of each other.

A new Bill of Rights will clearly define the State's rights over the individual, for the good of humanity, and will incorporate phraseology more reminiscent of George Orwell's *Animal Farm* than of a modern democratic state. Doublespeak will reach new standards of deception and, caught between the need to survive and blind obedience to 'God on Earth', the population will become willing accomplices in their own entrapment. The complaisant citizen will gain at one stroke religious certainty, food, clothing, shelter and employment in exchange for obedience to the law and the state – his every need will be provided for by the magic of Ahrimanic technology, all he has to sacrifice is his individual spiritual identity.

The legal, administrative, judicial and educational systems of all States reinforce and underpin the values, power and prestige of the ruling class – the New World Order, so long secretly in preparation by some of the financial and industrial leaders of our time, will have refined these concepts to perfection. The lure of material comfort, inherent in the new technology, will act as the perfect bribe that ensures the silence of most potential rebels among the population. For those who do refuse to accept the new order, or have the temerity to question it, all the well-tried methods of coercion and terror will come into operation. All the lessons learnt by the totalitarian States of the past will be applied with full vigour with the willing consent of the majority of the people in the name of God, who, like the German population during the Nazi era, will pretend that the death camps do not exist. But on this occasion the inmates will suffer in addition a religious inquisition as well as political persecution.

All who support the New World Order will be assured of comfortable material standards, good health care, education for their children and freedom from worry provided they accept the direction of the State in all aspects of their lives. Where you work, where you may live, when you may marry and how many children you will be permitted to bear will no longer be personal decisions, but will be decided at the discretion of the new world bureaucracy. Personal choice will not even be permitted in the area of employment. Direction of labour will be part of the new structure.

> He was given power to give breath to the image of the first beast, so that it could speak and cause all who refused to worship the image to be killed.
>
> He also forced everyone, small and great, rich and poor, free and slave, to receive a mark on his right hand or on his forehead, so that no one could buy or sell unless he had the mark which is the name of the beast or the number of his name.
>
> This calls for wisdom. If anyone has insight, let him calculate the number of the beast, for it is man's number. His number is 666.
>
> Revelation (New International Version): 13, verses 15–18

The mark of the beast has its immediate precursor today, the credit card, with all the computerized technology of personal records, inquiry and control that accompanies it.

The ambition and greed for power of those whose long-term aim has been world government is such that they wish to have total control over every aspect of people's lives, not merely in the area of politics but especially in the realm of finance. In the lifetime of the Anti-Christ there will be no repetition of the turning over of the money tables in the Temple because the money changers themselves will be his greatest allies. Ahriman himself tempted Christ in the wilderness, challenging him to turn stones into bread, but failed. Yet Ahriman succeeded in seducing Judas to betray his Master for thirty pieces of silver, and ever since the power of money has been Satan's strongest weapon against humanity. Christ himself said clearly 'You cannot serve both God and Mammon.'

In attempting to visualize the sequence of events in the rise of the Anti-Christ, Vladimir Soloviev pictures a great Church Council in Jerusalem where the leaders of the Roman Catholic, Eastern Orthodox and Protestant Churches are called together for a reuniting of all Christian faiths in eternal allegiance to the Anti-Christ. Supposedly this takes place in the Temple which has been rebuilt on Mount Moriah to replace the Islam mosque of 'The Dome of the Rock' which stands there at the present time. It has been a Jewish tradition since the time of Maimonides in the Middle Ages that the Jewish Messiah will not appear until the Temple is rebuilt. It is not beyond the realms of possibility that such a council will be formed to inaugurate the birth of the New World Religion in which church leaders of all denominations including the Jews will be asked to swear eternal fidelity to the Two-Horned Beast in the disguise of Jesus Christ. The Dogma of the New World Religion will deny the individual human spirit. The intellect will be declared the highest faculty of the soul of man who is not capable of insight into the realms of spiritual existence after death. The salvation of the soul is to be sought in a geographical heaven hitched to the end of life as a reward for blind obedience to the New World Order and unquestioning worship of 'God on Earth'.

The wise and pious among the Jewish fraternity will be among the leaders of the spiritually aware of all faiths who will come together to form the most widespread and determined underground movement against the pernicious distortion of God-given spiritual values, represented by the edicts of the New World Order and the Anti-Christ.

The members of the underground will be those people from all walks of life who have entered upon a path of spiritual self-discovery in which they have united the rational mind and the new spiritual faculties to reveal the presence of the spiritual world; people who have begun to unveil the meaning of their personal destiny and accept with love the dictates of the individual human spirit in the service of the true aims of mankind. We have already described how the White Horse represented man's early consciousness in which he was an unknowing vessel of universal intelligence. And how the gradual descent of human consciousness was depicted by St John in three further stages symbolized by the Red, Black and Pale Horses, which progressively isolated mankind from the spiritual world.

Now amongst the leaders of worldwide passive resistance to the New World Order, leaders appear who have regained with self awareness the original sublime consciousness symbolized by the first appearance of the White Horse. Among them will be the reappearance on earth of St John himself, the Apostles, and the leading souls of the great spiritual movements throughout the ages including the Templars, the Grail Knights, the Cathars and the genuine Rosicrucians. In fact all those striving souls whom we have already described as contributing to the spontaneous undirected 'Aquarian Conspiracy'.

The penalty that will be paid by many of the new spiritual underground will be horrendous; the nearest parallel we have in our time is the fate meted out to the Jews during the Holocaust. The battle between the sword of the rider of the White Horse and the cohorts of the Great Dictator is not a battle in the conventional historical sense, but the more important age-old spiritual conflict between good and evil. And it will be at the same time a struggle by the spiritually enlightened to discover and establish the true spiritual and political direction for the future. This is the reality behind the reappearance of the rider of the White Horse and his spiritually inspired followers who are described in mythological symbolism by St John as overthrowing the global evil of the Great Dictator.

I saw heaven standing open and there before me was a white horse, whose rider is called Faithful and True. With justice he judges and makes war. His eyes are like blazing fire, and on his head are many crowns. He has a name written on him that no one but he himself knows. He is dressed in a robe dipped in blood, and his name is the Word of God. The armies of heaven were following him, riding on white horses and dressed in fine linen, white and clean. Out of his mouth comes a sharp sword with which to strike down the nations.
Revelation (New International Version): 19, verses 11—15

According to the Revelation good will triumph over evil and the global reign of the Great Dictator will last 'forty-two months'. Yet presumably, as the soul aspiring to global dictatorship will only achieve this in a gradual build-up of power, State by State, the entire period leading up to and including the time of actual world domination will not exceed two decades. The rise to power of this second appearance of the Leviathan will mirror the events of the previous occasion when he possessed the soul of Adolf

Hitler. Although in the case of the Nazi era the appalling policy of genocide was not implemented for eight years, persecution of dissenting minorities and the denial of human rights started at the very inception of the regime. This should make it clear to everybody that it is not in forty years' time that the essential dilemma must be resolved, but right now. The spiritual battle between good and evil, which will culminate in these terrible coming apocalyptic events, has already begun.

Now when we are standing at the very threshold of the spiritual world a great personal and irrevocable decision must be made. The symbol which should help you make your decision, one way or another, is the Spear of Longinus. On the one side it will become the very emblem of the World Dictator who will claim it as his own talisman of global power. On the other it is the symbol of the redemptive sacrificial ritual of love at Golgotha and the inspiration of all who seek to tread the pathway to spiritual freedom. In the great apocalyptic battle between good and evil this vital decision cannot be postponed –

Whose side are **you** on?

THE END

EPILOGUE

Since *The Spear of Destiny* was first published in 1972, hundreds of thousands of people have made a special visit to the Hofburg to see the Holy Lance that is associated with so strange a legend. It is conceivable that many readers of this book will also wish to gain a closer acquaintance with this spiritually charged relic of the Supreme Sacrifice at Golgotha, and that among them will be two young men that we have called the Great Dictator and the Anti-Christ.

For a little while longer the Spear of Destiny will continue to rest on a faded red dais within an open leather case in the Habsburg treasure house in the Hofburg in Vienna. It is still on view to the public from Monday to Saturday from 9 a.m. to 6 p.m. Admission is free.

Why not make a special trip to see the Spear of Destiny

– while you still can!

BIBLIOGRAPHY

Alperovitz, Dr Gar: *Atomic Diplomacy.*
Aron, R: *Introduction to the Philosophy of History*, London, 1961.
Assmann, Kurt: *Deutsche Schicksalsjahre*, Wiesbaden, 1950.
Barnaby, Dr Frank (Ed.): *The Gaia Peace Atlas*, Pan Books, 1988.
Bartz, Karl: *Als der Himmel brannte*, Hanover, 1956.
Bible, The, King James Version and New International Version.
Blavatsky, H.P.: *Isis Unveiled*, Theosophical U.P., 1972.
Boehme, Jacob: *Signature of All Things*, Trs. Clarke, Cambridge, 1982.
Boethius: *The Consolation of Philosophy*, Penguin Books, 1969.
Bormann, Martin: *The Bormann Letters: The Private Correspondence between Martin Bormann and his wife, January 1943 to April 1945.* Weidenfeld & Nicolson, 1954.
Boyle, Stewart & Ardill, John: *The Greenhouse Effect*, London, 1989.
Bullock, Alan: *Hitler – A Study in Tyranny.* Penguin, 1969.
Butler, Dom C.: *Western Mysticism*, London, 1947.
Capra, Fritjof: *The Tao of Physics*, Fontana, 1983.
Capra, Fritjof: *The Turning Point*, Fontana, 1983.
Cohn, N: *The Pursuit of the Millennium*, Paladin, 1970.
Cronin, Vincent: *Napoleon*, Penguin, 1982.
Davy, John: *On Hope, Evolution and Change*, Hawthorn Press, 1985.
Diels, Rudolph: *Lucifer ante Portas*, Stuttgart, 1950.
de Chardin, Pierre Teilhard: *The Future of Man*, London, 1964.
———— *The Phenomenon of Man*, New York, 1959.
———— *Le Milieu Divin*, Paris, 1957.
Egyptian Book of the Dead, The
Eliade, M: *The Myth of the Eternal Return*, Tr. W.R. Trask, Penguin, 1989.
Evans, Hilary: *Alternate States of Consciousness*, Aquarian Press, 1989.
Faithful Thinker, The: An Anthology, Hodder & Stoughton.
Ferguson, Marilyn: *The Aquarian Conspiracy*, Paladin, 1982.
Fingarette, H: *The Self in Transformation*, London, 1961.
Fortune, Dion: *The Esoteric Orders and Their Work*, Aquarian Press, 1987.
Fox, Matthew: *The Original Blessing*, Bear & Co., U.S., 1987.
Goerlitz, W: *The History of the German General Staff*, U.S., 1953.
Goethe, J.W. von: *Faust . . . Translated in the original metre by Bayard Taylor*, Strahan & Co., 1871.
Hanfstangl, Ernst: *Adolf Hitler – The Missing Years*, London, 1957.
Hegel, G.W.F.: *Lectures on the Philosophy of History*, Tr. J. Sibree, Dover Pub, 1956.

—— *The Philosophy of Right*, Tr. T.M. Knox, Oxf. U.P. (N.Y.), 1967.
Howe, Ellic: *Urania's Children*, William Kimber, 1970.
Ibuse, Masuji: *Black Rain*, Bester translation, New York, 1985.
Jaynes, Julian: *The Origin of Consciousness in the Breakdown of the Bicameral Mind*, Houghton Mifflin, 1982.
Jones, Michael: *Nuclear Energy – a Spiritual Perspective*, Floris Books, 1983.
Jung, C.J: *Essays on the Science of Mythology*, London, 1956.
Jungk, Robert: *Brighter than a Thousand Suns*, Penguin, 1970.
Laing, R.D: *The Divided Self*, Penguin, 1970.
Lehrs, Ernst: *Man or Matter*, Faber & Faber, 1951.
Lovelock, J: *Gaia: A New Look At Life On Earth*, O.U.P., 1982.
—— *The Ages of Gaia*, O.U.P., 1988.
Marcuse, H: *One-dimensional Man*, Ark Pub., 1986.
McClure, Kevin: *The Evidence for Visions of the Virgin Mary*, Aquarian Press, 1983.
Michelet, J: *Satanism and Witchcraft*, Citadel Press, 1987.
Morizot: *The Templars*, The Anthroposophical Publishing Co., 1932.
Myers, Norman (Ed.): *The Gaia Atlas Of Planet Management*, Pan Books, 1985.
Pauwels, Louis and Jaques Bergier: *The Dawn of Magic*, Gibbs & Phillips, 1963.
Peck, M.S.: *The People of the Lie*, Century, 1988.
—— *The Road Less Travelled*, Century, 1988.
Pole, Wellesley Tudor: *The Silent Road*, Spearman, 1960.
Rauschning, Hermann: *The Revolution of Nihilism . . . Translated by E. W. Dickes*, William Heinemann, 1939.
—— *Time of Delirium*, New York, 1946.
Ravenscroft, Trevor: *The Cup of Destiny*, Samuel Weiser Inc., York Beach.
Shakespeare, William: *The Complete Works*, O.U.P., 1987.
Shepherd, A.P.: *Scientist of the Invisible:* Introduction to the Life and Work of Rudolf Steiner, Floris, 1983.
Soloviev, Vladimir: *The Philosophy of the Organic.*
Southern, R.W.: *The Making of The Middle Ages*, Cresset Lib, 1987.
Spretnak, Charlene: *The Spiritual Dimensions of Green Politics*, Bear Pub. U.S., 1987.
Stein, Walter Johannes: *The Ninth Century, World History in the Light of The Holy Grail*, Temple Lodge, 1988.
Steiner, Dr. Rudolf: *Das Goetheanum*, weekly journal for Anthroposophy, founded by Rudolf Steiner, General Anthroposophical Society.
—— *From Jesus to Christ*, 11 lectures, October 1911, Rudolph Steiner Press, 1973.
—— *Goethe's World View*, New York, Mercury Press, ca 1985.
—— *Knowledge of the Higher Worlds and its Attainment*, Anthroposophical Press, 1986.
—— *Lectures on the Gospel of St. John*, delivered in March, 1906; May,

1908; July, 1909; Temple Lodge Press, 1980; Anthroposophical Press, 1982; 1984.

————— *Macrocosm and Microcosm*, Rudolf Steiner Press, 1986.

————— *Man as a Symphony of the Creative World*, 12 lectures, Dornach, 1923.

————— *Theory of Knowledge Based on Goethe's World Conception*, Anthroposophical Press, 1979.

————— *The Etherization of the Blood: the Participation of the Etheric Christ in Human Evolution*, Rudolf Steiner Publishing Co., 1971.

————— *The Philosophy of Spiritual Activity*, New York, Steinerbooks, 1980; also Rudolf Steiner Publications, 1980.

————— *The Course of My Life*, Anthroposophical Press, 1986.

————— *The Riddles of Philosophy*, Anthroposophical Press, 1973.

Summers, M: *Witchcraft and Black Magic*, 1946.

Trevor-Roper, H.R.: *The Last Days of Hitler*, 3rd edn, London, 1956.

Trevelyan, George: *A Vision of the Aquarian Age*, Coventure, 1977.

Velikovsky, Immanuel: *Earth in Upheaval*, Sphere, 1974.

Wachsmuth, Gunter: *Etheric Formative Forces in Cosmos, Earth and Man. Re-incarnation*, The Anthroposophical Publishing Co., 1932.

Winkler, Frans: *Man, the Bridge of Two Worlds*, Hodder & Stoughton, 1960.

Wilson, Bryan: *Magic and The Millennium*, Paladin, 1975.

INDEX

AIDS epidemic, 211
Academy in Alexandria, 124; of
    Hades, 122; of Jundi-Shapur,
    123–33, 143, 200, 204, 220; of
    Jundi-Shapur, ruins of, 128–9;
    of Nautical Discovery at
    Sagras, 67; Platonic, 74
Acid rain, 175
Acropolis, 105
Adepts, black, 80–1; skilled, 80
Aeronautical engineering, 35
Aerosols, CFC gases are now
    banned from use in, 179
Aeschylus, 116
Afghanistan invasion, the, 201
Africa, drought and famine in,
    210
Age of Discovery, 55
Ahab, 112
Ahriman, 33–4, 82, 127–9, 204;
    anticipating the birth in the
    flesh of, 220; himself tempted
    Christ in the wilderness, 225;
    is the spirit of dissemblance,
    211; succeeded in seducing
    Judas, 225; the birth of *A*. will
    be anticipated and attended
    by initiates, 221; the date of
    the birth of, 210; the fallen
    Seraphim, 205; the atom
    bomb as the instrument of,
    158; the physical birth of, 210;
    who has united science and
    religion, 222; will be revered
    as the returning Christ, 222;
    will declare himself as the
    reappearance of Jesus Christ,
    211; will deliver his entire
    global flock to the Great
    Dictator, 222
Ahrimanic impulses are clearly at
    work within American society,
    160
Ahura Mazdā, 44
Akashic Record, 105, 205

Alamogordo, New Mexico on
    16 July 1945, 151
Albertus Magnus, 132
Alfred the Great, 24, 25, 107–8
Alperovitz, Dr Gar, author of
    Atomic Diplomacy, 149
Alternative sciences, 196
American Constitution, 40, 80
Ammonius Saccas, 116
Andropov, Yuri, 194
Anaxagorus, 124
Anglo-Saxon Chronicle, the, 107
Angry brigade, the, 163
Animal Farm, George Orwell's,
    223
Annas, 200
Anti-Christ, 3, 13–14, 133, 204,
    210–11, 220–5; Soloviev's, 13;
    The Great Dictator as the
    essential partner to the rise of
    the, 220; the prophesied
    appearance of the, 200
Apocalypse, the, 3, 5, 8, 12–13,
    15, 32, 40, 42, 54, 61, 69, 75,
    78; advances entirely in
    rhythms of seven, 207; first
    phase of the twentieth
    century, 10; Four Horses of, 6,
    16, 46
    Black Horse, 18–19, 21; the
        beginning of the epoch of
        the, 54, 60; Pale Horse, 6,
        16, 20–1, 30, 36, 137;
        apocalyptic reality facing
        mankind under the
        shadow of the, 165; Life in
        the shadow of the, 122,
        137, 153; transition from
        the age of the Black Horse
        to the emergence of the,
        137; whose rider is Death
        and whose following are
        the hosts of hell, 137, 167;
        Red Horse, 18, 21, 45;
        White Horse, 16–17, 45;

233

Trevor Ravenscroft was born in England in 1921. He was educated at Repton and Sandhurst Military College before serving as a Commando officer in World War II.

He was captured on a raid which attempted to assassinate Field Marshal Rommel in North Africa and was a POW in Germany from 1941 to 1945, escaping three times but each time being recaptured.

After the war he studied at St. Thomas's Hospital, later becoming a journalist. He studied history under Dr. Walter Johannes Stein for twelve years, carrying out extensive research for this book. Before his death in 1989, he also lectured on history in London and Edinburgh.

Tim Wallace-Murphy was born in Galway, Ireland. After completing military service he studied medicine from 1953 to 1958. However, he felt unsuited to this vocation and in 1960 set off to travel around Africa and Europe. He returned in 1970 and settled in Devon where he resumed his academic career, reading sociology, politics, economics, and psychology. He now works as a freelance writer and lecturer, and is actively involved with several charity organizations.